D0371847

THE ENGLISH GENTLEMAN
Images and Ideals
in
Literature and Society

DAVID CASTRONOVO

THE
ENGLISH
GENTLEMAN

IMAGES AND IDEALS
IN
LITERATURE AND SOCIETY

UNGAR   NEW YORK

1987
The Ungar Publishing Company
370 Lexington Avenue, New York, N.Y. 10017

Printed in the United States of America

Designed by Tom Mellers

Library of Congress Cataloging-in-Publication Data

Castronovo, David.
The English gentleman.
Bibliography: p.
Includes index.
1. English literature—History and criticism.
2. Men in literature.   3. Social ethics in
literature.   4. Manners and customs in literature.
5. Great Britain—Gentry—History.   6. England—
Social life and customs.   I. Title.
PR151.M46C37   1987   820'.9'355   87-5084
ISBN 0-8044-2105-6

In Memory of
Loretta and David Oliver

CONTENTS

INTRODUCTION

This book has its origins in a fascination with *Great Expectations,* Charles Dickens's late novel about a village boy named Pip who discovers the allure of being a gentleman and only casts off his illusions when he reaches the brink of tragedy. A misused orphan facing a life of tedium as a blacksmith, Pip is magically catapulted into London life by an unknown patron and cherishes the notion of marrying Estella, an icy young lady whom he knew as a child. I first read the novel in the late 1950s—at a time when I was old enough to fall in love with Estella, feel that Pip had found one of life's main chances, and realize that Dickens had a powerful hold on the enduring theme of man's struggle to be superior to the circumstances of birth. The atmosphere of Satis House—the gothic property of Miss Havisham where Pip first meets Estella—also put a charge on Dickens's subject; with its gloomy interiors, bizarre owner, ruined garden, and tormenting enchantress, it invested Dickens's conflict with glamour and grotesqueness.

Pip—the boy who wanted to be a gentleman to show Estella what he was worth and to escape from the hideous life of his class—remains as the prototypical modern yearner: while his identity later became complicated by my adult sense of his petty cruelties, his discontent and ambition seem to be permanently valuable features of many people's lives. How many men and women are satisfied with the narrow confines of their early years? How many have fantasized about a more generous and attractive life? *Great Expectations* is a richly textured critique of genteel fantasy—complete with new clothes, London lodgings, vain hopes about a woman, and a disaster. In its ironic way, it supplies all the illusions and all the recognitions.

Dickens's book exerts a complex kind of pressure because of its ambivalence. It stands as a novelistic fork in the road—directing the reader to the gentleman's uselessness and also to his desire for significance. We experience the protagonist's frustrated love, damaged friendship, futile expense of vital powers—only to feel the pleasures of freedom and release, the sense that there is something finer and better than being resigned to a dull provincial existence. The ideals of the gentleman begin in these contradictory possibilities: at times nasty or noble, snobbish or generous, the gentleman—whether a fictional personage or an actual man—seems to hold within his mystique many of mankind's finer aspirations and baser instincts. Grasping, acquisitive, arrogant, selfish—such a string of charges can easily be matched with references to the gentleman's integrity, love of diversity and liberty, high moral sense, and responsibility.

The pages ahead are meant to set down some of the irony and variety that the ideal has accumulated in English literature and life. While the gentleman is no longer a central figure in culture, the issues of status, power, self-assertion, and self-cultivation never seem to disappear. I offer the models and images of this book in the hope that they contain within them some kernel of value for a world that does not talk much about the gentleman, but has yet to act without reference to his virtues and his defects. Dickens's Pip yearned for much that we still desire. And who can be quite sure of having cast off Pip's ambitions and dreams of fulfillment based on social position? The story of a common village boy who wants to be a gentleman stands not only as a fable about falling from innocence but also as one of the most compelling projects of literary protagonists and real people in the last five hundred years.

THE ENGLISH GENTLEMAN

PART ONE

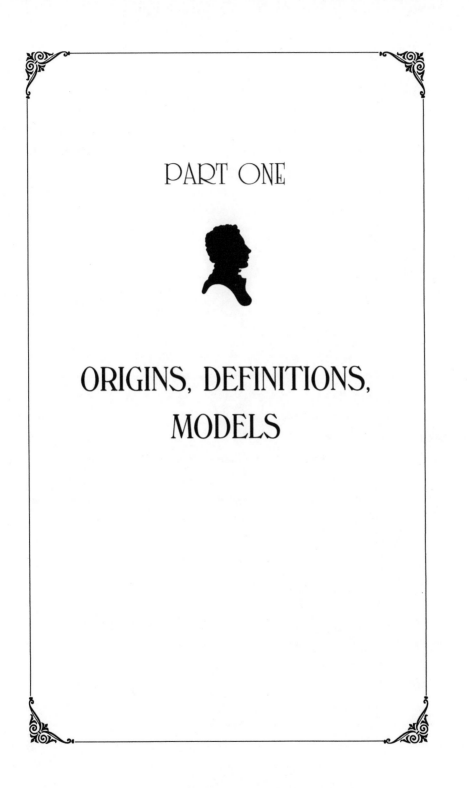

ORIGINS, DEFINITIONS, MODELS

THE WORD "GENTLEMAN" has done more than its share for English literature and history: it has helped to describe such varying personalities as Christ and Satan, Beau Brummell and Captain Cuttle, the Duke of Wellington and Oliver Twist, Lord Chesterfield and Tom Brown; it has been subjected to every indignity and abuse that a word can endure; it has followed the contours of an evolving society while managing to go off on every fashionable tangent; it has been redefined, revolutionized, reshaped, discarded, and also reappropriated; it has been given little rest in the past two hundred years and has experienced a painful old age, filled with the company and comfort of vulturous relations ready to fight over the inheritance; it will dissolve perhaps with this century and its property will be broken up, divided by professionals and intellectuals, the rich and the powerful; its ghost—the nine letters it is spelled with— will appear, perhaps even frequently, evoking laughter rather than hostility or approbation. For traditionalists, the word may continue to carry real meaning; for others, it will be a dim reminder of life-styles and values that never quite disappear.

This book—devoted to one of civilization's oldest status terms— seeks to piece together the fragments of a way of living, to reassemble the components of a socioeconomic function that formed a once intelligible and meaningful design on the face of English literature and social life. The gentleman's influence was never "taken for granted," was never "beyond question" in the realm of literary culture; there were always those who wanted gentlemanly power destroyed, who questioned gentle blood and manners, who sought preeminence for other forms of personal distinction. Yet the ideal of the gentleman—irrespective of the treatment it received—was always central when questions of who shall rule, who shall serve, and who shall be emulated arose. The gentleman in Hippolyte Taine's words contains "the history of English Society"[1]: his rise and fall parallels the history of property and privilege that is the bedrock of a national life. Although the whole story of the gentleman is beyond our scope and purpose, the following pages are an attempt to construct a series of models, to set down theory and practice, and to evolve ideal types that describe the major uses of the word "gentleman" in literature and life.

I have also viewed English gentlemen as a tribe; with their ancestor worship, self-protective habits, fear of outsiders, self-referring customs, rituals, and prohibitions, they seem like nothing so much as a band of exotic survivors of the modern world who have something valuable to tell about the conduct of life, and much to warn us about as well. As these survivors move farther from the center of our culture, their folkways need to be recalled if we are to gauge our present position properly.

THE GENTLEMAN OF BIRTH   1

The essential building block is the word itself. The range of definitions and distinctions must begin with the denotative value of the word
gens. Behind the word gens is *genere,* which is the etymological root
from which a cluster of words emerge. The member of the tribe (gens)
was the man who was well begotten (*genere*). The Latin word *gentilis,*
meaning belonging to a good family, is an offshoot of gens and appears
in Old French as *gentil*—highborn, noble. The next step in the etymological opening out is the Old French *gentil hom,* which begins to
appear in English as "gentile man" (1275) and "gentil men" (1297).
Also from the Old French *gentil* and partly from the Old French *gent*
(meaning wellborn) comes the English word gentry, which begins to
appear during the late fourteenth century. The word gentility came
into English and also denoted gentle birth. Genteel was the adjective
that later corresponded to the word gentleman: originally in the sixteenth century it denoted good birth; its connotation of respectability
came much later. The idea of the gentleman thus had its roots in words
that denoted good birth and membership in a family. The idea opens
out from the whole notion of the tribe and family: being of a "known"
family is what is meant by having gentle blood. Nobility means nota-
bility; to be ignoble is to be unknown. Nobility and gentility were
synonymous terms right through the Renaissance; they both denoted
men of ancestry. "Gentlemen be those, whom their blood and race doth
make noble or known."[2] A problem arises concerning the word "known."
Who was known and how? This question, unfortunately, is likely to
lead to confusing responses: for the Herald's College—that ominous
fountainhead of all legal gentility in England—sold certificates and coats
of arms to families who were established. These families were known
ultimately for prowess of arms and proximately for their landholdings

and longtime residence and maintenance of a certain style of life. What may seem vague to us about gentle birth was evidently not as vague to Renaissance Englishmen: the Herald's College set up a series of visitations[3] between 1529 and 1686 to decide on matters of gentlemanly status. Every thirty years the "king of arms" traveled the countryside; he confirmed those gentlemen who were "armigerous"—who had the legal right to display a coat of arms and to sign themselves "Gent"— and degraded by public proclamation made by the town crier those who were pretenders.[4] The litigation generated by this process was enormous and opened whole areas of dispute and bitterness. For the word "gentleman" divided society in two: it was a formal rank and even into our own time heraldic specialists have boldly, if somewhat absurdly, maintained its absolute integrity. On one side of society were the "wretched 'plebians': on the other side were 'the gentlemen of coat armour.' "[5]

The arbitrary character of this distinction was summed up early in the history of the idea. John Ball's couplet is often cited:

> When Adam delved and Eve span
> Who was then the gentleman?[6]

Yet the extravagance of the mists-of-antiquity theories of the gentleman were only matched by their importance. The passion for ancestors is a recurrent theme in English literature and history: while Oxford claims King Alfred for its founder, Cambridge claims King Arthur.[7] Pride of ancestry, according to Professor Lawrence Stone, had for its prime purpose the task of social integration, of welding a homogeneous group from diverse origins.[8] And the heralds were willing to go to great lengths to help certain men to clothe their "social nackedness"[9]: to make them gentlemen of blood the heralds often began with Noah in tracing a genealogy. The main point is that one must claim status and be accepted in order to enjoy it. There were always back roads to achieving rank; gentlemanly status—the coat-of-arms itself—had to be purchased. The question of who could do the purchasing was vague: it almost seems as if the Herald's College made its visitations in an attempt to deny the great single fact of English social life—its ever-increasing, mysterious fluidity. The idea of gentle blood lasted right into the nineteenth century as a test of status, but the gentleman's future was vaguer in terms of reference than even the mists-of-time. For people frequently came from "nowhere" into the ranks of gentility: yeomen and merchants became rich, began to live in a gentlemanly style, became accepted, purchased coat armor, and were counted as gentlemen. There were those who were stopped in their ascent, there were those pretenders who were unmasked. But the door was open: the question is how and why were people stopped from entering.

But before continuing on to the question of fluidity, we must attempt to construct our first model—the man of blood, the Herald's Gentleman, as he is often called. *Bailey's Dictionary* (1707) gives the lineaments of the portrait: a gentleman is defined as "one who receives his nobility from his ancestors, and not from the gift of any prince or state."[10] This definition involves the distinction between a man of blood and a man of rank. The sovereign conferred the ranks in the peerage, but even in his name the Herald's College could not "make" a man of blood: ancestry was supposedly recognized by the college. The Herald's Gentleman was thus ideally a gentleman before a patent of arms was conferred on him. (And, of course, there were those men of blood and ancestry who ignored the Herald's College altogether but who were recognized as gentlemen in their locality because they were men who were "known.") The gentleman's status, in other words, was not open to on-the-spot creation. It was a rank, but not a rank that a sovereign conferred. James I's old nurse supposedly asked him to make her son a gentleman: he replied that he could make him a baronet, but that God almighty couldn't make him a gentleman.[11] Francis Bacon wrote that "new nobility is but the act of power, but ancient nobility is the act of time." The condition of the gentleman of blood was inexorable in theory: neither conduct nor achievement nor rank in the peerage could augment or diminish his gentility. Samuel Johnson defined the gentleman as "a man of ancestry" and dismissed all other considerations as "whimsical." The only other condition that can and must be affixed to the portrait is the holding of an estate: the Herald's Gentleman was ipso facto a man of property. Sir Walter Elliot in *Persuasion* is the quintessential man of birth and property. He requires that the word "gentleman" be defined along the strictest lines. A country curate has been referred to as a gentleman and he replies:

Wentworth? Oh, ay—Mr. Wentworth, the curate of Monford. You misled me by the term *gentleman*. I thought you were speaking of some man of property: Mr. Wentworth was nobody, I remember; quite unconnected: nothing to do with the Stafford family. One wonders how the names of many of our nobility became so common.

Sir Walter's conception bordered on comicality, if not ludicrousness, by the time of the Regency. For Jane Austen's art—and the society which it in part reflected—was moving away from caste and exclusiveness toward a revitalized and more inclusive form of gentility. Yet, for every movement forward in the development of the idea of the gentleman, there was likely to be a backward jolt: the notion of blood as the primary component in the gentleman's condition never died. In a recent philosophical treatment of the gentleman in Anthony Trollope's novels, Shirley Letwin argues that the idea of birth is the least important criterion for gentility because "no man in England can safely boast of his ancestors." While this generalization is true even for the proudest families, it neglects all the insistence and fantasy connected with blood.[12] English literature and history is charged with excitement about the matter of "who's who"—and no amount of moralizing ever really destroys the magic component of pedigree.

In 1828 Sir James Lawrence published a volume called *On the Nobility of the British Gentry:* no Herald could have been any more emphatic about blood as the sole test of gentility; Sir James never entertained the notion that a gentleman could be anything but a man of ancestry.[13] He is a kind of Sir Walter Elliot in the world of fact—always warning his readers against the incursion of base pretenders, always ready to say that politeness in a man does not make him a gentleman. And, like Sir Walter Elliot with his copy of the Baronetage, he is forever asserting pride of ancestry, forever making invidious comparisons between Continental noblemen and English gentlemen.

But one need not wait until the nineteenth century to see how blood literally shaped the lives of men and set a limit to their aspirations. Classic bids for status and arrogant rebuffs have been the English way of social life at least since the Renaissance. One Richard Barker claimed gentility on three counts during the reign of Henry VIII: first, he was steward of the courts of the Duke of Buckingham; second, he was married to a knight's daughter; third, he had arms from the Herald's College.[14] His coat of arms was "a hunde barkying stondyng in a shyld." The judges laughed him out of court—his father was a turner. (Significantly, the author of the 1902 article telling of Barker's fate is in concurrence with Renaissance society's judgment: he considers the barking hound very humorous and regards poor Barker as an annoying bounder.)

Blood, in fact, had an almost mystical significance. It had a vague but real biological component: the "born" man was good breeding stock;

to be "utterly unborn" was to begin life with a narrow range of possibilities for growth and good breeding.[15] To those who believed in birth, there was a great deal at stake in keeping the criterion valid. For birth was an awe-inspiring pact arranged by fate between a few thousand men and the real property of a nation. Thorsten Veblen dryly called gentle blood "blood which has been ennobled by protracted contact with accumulated wealth or unbroken prerogative."[16] And it was from this notion of protracted contact with land and enjoyment of privilege that the historical fact of a class of gentry grew. This class of gentry is frequently confused with the idea of the gentleman: they are interrelated but not interchangeable.

The class of gentry originally denoted the elder and younger sons of knights—esquires and gentlemen respectively. The term "gentleman," when it refers to a member of a class of gentry, is a designation of rank. Sir George Sitwell maintains that in this formal sense no one "ever described himself or was described by others as a gentleman before 1413."[17] The medievalist Sylvia Thrupp dates the term from 1413 because a statute of that year (Henry V, c. 5) required the giving of the "estate, degree or mystery" of the defendant in all writs and appeals concerning personal action and in all indictments.[18] Sir George—who made the same point in 1902, also claiming that there were "no gentlemen in the Middle Ages," only nobles and esquires—makes a fascinating case for the "rise of the gentry." "Gentil" before the first quarter of the fifteenth century meant noble: it did not denote a class of men apart from the nobility. The term "gentleman" gradually became a fashionable and meaningful label after Henry V's statute. In 1413 the "premier gentleman of England"—one "Robert Erdeswyke of Stafford, gentleman"—was charged with murder, assault, and robbery. (Professor Thrupp indicates that he was no anomaly: there was a class of "gentlemen" who were professional criminals in the fifteenth century.[19]) The word "gentleman" makes its next major appearance after Erdeswyke on a monument erected for John Daundelyon in 1445.[20] The first man returned to Parliament as a "gentleman" was William Eston in January 1447.[21] All Chaucer's talk of "gentil" men is quite apart from this very definite idea of a class of men who needed a term to describe their relation to the social hierarchy. The modern, unformalized idea of the gentleman got mixed up with this class term.[22] This confusion should not blind us to the fact that members of the class of gentry need have no relation to morality or manners: they were a group of people committed to perpetuating themselves, to keeping estates intact, to finding places for their younger sons, to ruling the community and governing the nation.

As the wealth and complexity of English society increased, so did the ranks of its gentry. More money and more national activity meant more places for younger sons who would not be returned to the soil— to the ranks of the yeoman class—by inability to sustain the life-style of a gentleman. The life-style of a gentleman was an important criterion of gentility from the Renaissance onward. Sir Thomas Smith summed up its importance during Elizabeth's reign: "A gentleman must go like a gentleman."[23] The men who lived in a certain style and had ancestors, the men who abstained from manual labor and conceived of themselves as part of a web of hereditary relationship, were an eternal order; nobility meant permanence[24]—and it was forever, as Peter Laslett has put it. The gentlemen of England claimed that the Fifth Commandment gave them their privileges: superiors were fathers and blood gave society its only meaningful design.[25]

> The rich man in his castle,
> The poor man at his gate,
> God made them high and lowly
> And ordered each estate.[26]

This finally worked out to a national life where what Laslett calls "subsumption" was the social reality: one class of people "lived" for the rest of the community. Such a social condition provoked Henry Fielding's famous definition of "No Body": "All the people in Great Britain except about 1200."[27] The top of the pyramid—those belonging to the major and minor nobility, the ranks of duke through gentleman—was much larger by Fielding's time, but the point remains: gentlemen were the only somebodies. In his late novel *Little Dorrit* Dickens satirizes the situation by presenting the mentality of public figures who ignored the population. When one spoke of the "country," one necessarily avoided recognizing the claims of anyone but men of birth: "It was only clear that the question was all about John Barnacle, Augustus Stiltstalking, William Barnacle and Tudor Stiltstalking, Tom, Dick, or Harry Barnacle or Stiltstalking, because there was nobody else but mob."

The component of birth was so firmly affixed to the word "gentleman" that great and minor novelists were often unable to detach themselves and their characters from it. Dickens, the preeminent anatomist of nineteenth-century corruption and class oppression, spoke seriously of his father's "coat of arms"—this when his father's mother was a domestic servant and the father himself was a civil servant who had been imprisoned for debt! Dickens's bedazzlement gives a curiously factitious direction to a novel of protest like *Oliver Twist:* the story of the little pauper in the workhouse finally concerns being wellborn.

The novel gradually uncovers the facts of origins after it has dramatized the most important truth—the goodness of Oliver. At this point in Dickens's career, goodness and gentleness are wholly consonant with gentle origins: Dickens seems to be showing the reader that the "outcome" of the novel—the discovery of Oliver's true status as the son of a gentleman—is, for all the wonderful and amazing circumstances that lead to it, perfectly appropriate. It seems that Dickens is operating on two levels here: he is trying to demonstrate the trials of a little hero, all the degrading and notorious facts of Oliver's life in the workhouse and at Fagin's, but he is also dealing with the idea that Oliver's salvation from the underworld has a "rightness" and "reasonability" to it. It is difficult to deny that there is something false in the unfolding of Oliver's destiny; it appears that Dickens planned on making Oliver a gentleman from the beginning of the narrative, probably because of his personal fascination with the idea of blood.

In this attachment to birth, *Oliver Twist* has more in common with a second-rate novel like Mrs. Craik's *John Halifax, Gentleman* (1856) than with Dickens's own first-magnitude works. Both novels have a mechanical way of presenting the all-important fact of life—gentle origins. Mrs. Craik's work deals with the discovery of genteel origins and the rise to respectability and prosperity of a little laboring boy. John, like Oliver before him, was the ragged child whose personal qualities—his manners, his gentleness, his goodness—gave him his gentlemanly status in the eyes of many members of the small community of Norton Bury. The title "gentleman" is generally accorded to him not because his origins are known, but because his fellow citizens recognize the responsibility, decency, honesty, and straightforwardness of his behavior. His trials in the novel shed light on the questions dealt with in *Oliver Twist.* For John Halifax is subjected to tests of endurance: he has to prove his quality by meeting a series of challenges not unlike those that Oliver is confronted with. Halifax's gentility is constantly brought into question: his kindly employer Mr. Fletcher spurns the notion of John's genteel aspirations, tells the young man to be content with his station—that of the honest worker in a tannery. John replies with a declaration that tells us a good deal about the idea of birth; we learn that the gentleman is more than his circumstances, that he cannot be "explained" by his environment. He tells us that the tannery "is only my calling, not me. I—John Halifax—am just the same, whether in the tan yard or Dr. Jessop's drawing room. The one position cannot degrade, nor the other elevate me. I should not respect myself otherwise." Living according to all this is strikingly similar to what Max Weber meant by "pure value related conduct":

> the behavior of persons who, regardless of consequences, conduct themselves in such a way as to put into practice their convictions of what appears to them to be required by duty, honor, beauty, religiosity, piety, or the importance of a "cause," no matter what its goal.

Both John Halifax and Oliver Twist live without regard to "consequences" (in John's case public opinion, in Oliver's danger); they both act out their convictions of what is honorable. We see that the idea of the gentleman impinges on another area—the whole idea of the elected soul or spirit. The abiding qualities of the gentleman of blood for John and Oliver cannot be altered by circumstances: like elected souls, they cannot be lowered by circumstances and cannot be stopped in their mission to be honorable because nobility of character is unaffected by the vicissitudes of life. They both wait to be "recognized": for the world to see them as gentlemen. John, of course, knows about "who he is"; yet Oliver, in a sense, acts as if he knew about his origins also. Throughout the narrative, he is more than a little boy: his every action bespeaks the idea of the little-gentleman-waiting-for-his-birthright.

This special status need not be thought of as a result of naked expropriation and conspiracy; gentlemanly position was conceded and acquiesced to according to what Walter Bagehot has described as the "politics of deference."[28] The born gentleman's almost mystical hold on the minds of the less privileged sometimes even takes the form of superstition: the country people at Sheringham, according to Derek Hudson, thought the gaze of a gentleman was a cure for disease.[29] F. M. L. Thompson sums up the attitude of ordinary people to gentlemen, an attitude that must have helped to preserve whatever social equilibrium existed in England. Those without notable origins "while denouncing it [the gentry] as functionless, privileged and parasitic, envied and sought to emulate it as the embodiment of all that was admirable in taste, manners and civilized living."[30] Men of family and property were *the* social standard. This, of course, was not unique to England. Baldassare

Castiglione's perfect courtier had to be a man of birth not only because birth kept him emulating his ancestors, but more importantly because gentle blood won popular favor. The people demanded and trusted men of ancestry as their governors. Castiglione's influence on English thought was enormous; Thomas Hoby's translation brought this influence into the mainstream of English Renaissance courtesy literature. But Continental theorizing on the question of gentility was outstripped by English reality in one significant respect: the English gentleman— for all his privileges—was not a member of a caste; his station entitled him to no legal immunities; his condition—his style of life, his coat armor, his land—could all be aspired to (and bought) by those below him. The ranks of English society were open; unknown men could found families. Men deferred to the gentleman because English society was built on a series of "removable inequalities."[31] While the man in the manor house may have felt his station to be fixed and eternal, there was no doubt about the fact that he could fall and others could rise. Once we have erected our first model—the Herald's Gentleman—it can be taken apart by the paradoxes of English life: men of birth were a class apart, but this exclusiveness had no ultimate legal sanction. No one, with the exception of the pauper, was above the law's reach or below its protection.[32]

Yet the concept of blood was difficult to remove from lives that it once touched. The "born" man—or even the man who lived on illusions of gentle birth—was somehow always destined to reckon with this compelling fact. Henry Kingsley created a character in his novel *Ravenshoe* who discovers that he is not the gentleman he thought he was; with the discovery it is almost impossible for Ravenshoe to continue thinking of himself as a person. Witness also Dickens's Alfred Jingle in *Pickwick Papers,* an insouciant and down-at-the-heels rogue who "plays" the role of gentleman and uses the lingo of the aristocracy to astonish and impress the middle-class types around him. With his "indescribable air of jaunty impudence and perfect self possession," he puts down people as skillfully as the genuine article like Sir Walter Elliot. He succeeds in remaining on top—until his fraudulence catches up with him and he winds up in the Fleet Prison, miserable and penniless. But even here, the parlance of the born gentleman is pathetically on his lips as he introduces himself: "Alfred Jingle, of No Hall, Nowhere."

THE GENTLEMAN
OF WEALTH

2

For all the self-consciousness of men of ancestry, they were pervasive models rather than implacable forces. Alexis de Tocqueville explains the full consequences of the conception of the English gentleman: he draws out all that is foreshadowed by and contained in the lack of legal immunities for the gentry. Comparing England with the Continent he finds that England is distinguished by:

> the ease with which it has opened its ranks . . . in general the aristocracy had everything at its disposal. But, with great riches, anybody could hope to enter into the rank of the aristocracy. Furthermore, since everybody could hope to become rich, especially in such a mercantile country as England, a peculiar position arose in that their privileges, which raised such feelings against the aristocrats of other countries, were the things that most attached the English to theirs. As everybody had the hope of being among the privileged, the privileges made the aristocracy, not more hated, but more valued.[1]

Tocqueville puts his finger on the key agent of social mobility—wealth. The fact that anybody could make money, buy real property, sell a prosperous business in the City, and retire to the country was an overwhelming reality of English life. The merchant class was abused and sneered at, but never stigmatized. The Russian merchant was a merchant in law, forbidden to buy land; the English merchant was the man who could become *The Spectator*'s Sir Andrew Freeport—an eminently respectable man, Sir Roger's friend, a gentleman. Lawrence Stone has described English society's capacity for absorption and integration:

> The measure of the resiliency of a class structure is its ability to absorb new families of different social origins and convert them to the values and ways of life of the social group into which they are projected.[2]

This is the process by which the rich man becomes the gentleman.

But before discussing the second model—the gentleman of wealth and substance, the gentleman as rich man—we might backtrack a moment by listening to what a commercial man, Daniel Defoe, had to say by way of definition about gentle blood and the gentleman:

> A person Born (for there lies the essence of Quality) of some known or Ancient Family, whose Ancestors have at least for some time been rais'd above the class of Mechanics. If we examine for how long it must be that is a dangerous Inquiry, we dive too deep, and may indeed strike at the Root of both the Gentry and Nobility; for all must begin somewhere, and would be traced to some less Degree in their original than will suit the vanity of the Day. It is enough therefore that we can derive for a Line of two or three generations, or perhaps less.[3]

Here the investigation of ancestral claims is called a dangerous inquiry: new men interpret the whole process of familial self-assertion as a risky business, one that is likely to yield the conclusion that Veblen's "protracted contact" is a vague generality or better yet that the making of a gentleman can be accelerated, that gentility can be distilled in a generation or two. The point is that gentility has shifted from condition to process: the gentleman can be manufactured; the mists of time have given way to the smell of industry. Meanwhile, the gentleman of blood and the new gentleman exist side by side: the Renaissance called the latter into being, but he by no means supplanted the gentleman of blood; he was rather an advance on the idea of birth—an idea that obviously was contracted and circumscribed by definition. The new gentleman certainly partook (or hoped to partake) of the official trappings of the man of birth. But William Harrison in his 1577 *Description of Britain* showed that indeed the Herald's College offered only trappings. The gentleman "shall for money have a coat and arms bestowed on him by the heralds (who in the character of the same do pretend antiquity, service and many gay things) and thereunto being made so good cheap, shall be called master, which is the title that men give to esquires and gentlemen, and reputed for a gentleman ever after."[4] Gentlemen are made "so good cheap": the Herald's College, rather than being seen as the repository of ancient honor and gentility, has taken on the aspect of an industry house.

By the Renaissance this manufacture of new men had already blurred the distinctions inherent in the notion of gentleman as a definite rank; the word denoted a rank, but its members were not fixed, not frozen into caste. Protest against the inroads of new people was not infrequent within English society. Yet, for all its consequences in the drawing rooms of country houses, such protest could not arrest a process set in motion. Jane Austen's Mary Elliot in *Persuasion* could say she thought little of new creations, but the future actually belonged to men like her brother-in-law, men who had amassed fortunes in the professions and only had to bide their time for rank. Nevertheless, Sir Walter Elliot disliked the navy: "First, as being the means of bringing men of obscure birth into undue distinction, and raising men to honors which their fathers and grandfathers never dreamt of." This die-hard conception of gentility does not ultimately mean that much. For Frederick Wentworth was a naval officer whose claim to gentility was as good as Mary's.

Military service, however, was not the only road to gentility. From the Tudor period onward, the class of gentry was opening itself to men other than distinguished soldiers. By the sixteenth century the nobility had lost its traditional occupation—warfare.[5] England, in fact, did not fall into the rigidity that created an impoverished class of knights on the Continent. When feudalism could yield the gentleman no more, he abandoned its spirit, even if he kept its forms. For the style of life that was the hallmark of the man of birth had to be maintained: the arrogant poverty of a decayed warrior was never in high repute; the whole notion behind "the port, charge and countenance of a gentleman"[6] is a conception of prosperity and ease of circumstances attained without manual labor. In the sixteenth century the playwright Robert Greene capsuled the Englishman's attitude: "What is Gentry if wealth be wanting, but base servile beggery?"[7] Less than a hundred years later the author of *The Vale Royal of England* was even more emphatic: "Riches maketh Gentlemen in all countries of England,"[8] Poverty was a disgrace to a gentleman: even stiff-necked Sir Walter Elliot had to let Kellynch Hall, had to abandon his property rather than alter by retrenchment the reputation for hospitality and dignity that the house had enjoyed. Tocqueville even went so far as to claim that the English aristocracy was founded on wealth. In a letter he sums up his attitude: "The respect paid to wealth in England is enough to make one despair."[9]

Yet despair was only one part of his response to the self-sustaining, self-renewing quality of the English gentry. For Tocqueville also felt that wealth could be manipulated and gentlemanly power altered. During an interviewing session he backed his subject into a corner, made him concede that to destroy the aristocracy one must destroy its sources of wealth, its sinecures and livings. To threaten the sources of livelihood of younger sons—the Civil Service posts, the Church livings—

would be to remind their elder brothers that wealth, not ancestry, was their mainstay in the nineteenth century. Tocqueville felt that wealth could thus play a central role in the progress of democracy:

> I see democracy represented by a great army but one without a leader. These missing leaders are in the aristocracy itself, but they must be made to come forward. The rearguard of the aristocracy must become the vanguard of democracy, and so it will be if, without attacking the advantages of the nobles, you make things difficult for their sons and brothers.[10]

This process of making it difficult for aristocratic fathers to find places in government for their younger sons was in fact attempted by the Civil Service Reform of 1870. This reform threw open government service to candidates who could pass an examination. No real democratization occurred, however: the gentleman of wealth could send his sons to Oxford and Cambridge and so prepare them for an examination that was geared to men who had had a gentleman's education. Wealth, if not aristocratic connections, could still find a place for a younger son.

Tocqueville describes another situation where wealth is crucial in the maintenance of gentlemanly power. His brilliant suggestion for the retention of aristocratic power follows the contours of Victorian history: "I still persist in believing that if the aristocracy could form a compact body with all the other classes who have some hope of sharing its privileges, it would succeed in holding out, for nothing is more difficult than for a people to make a revolution all by itself."[11] This coalition was what G. K. Chesterton meant by the Victorian Compromise;[12] it blurred the lines of aristocracy and plutocracy in an attempt to retain privileges for men who respected and could sustain a certain style of life. This Compromise was a Victorian device, but it was part of a larger process in English history: it partook of the spirit of James I's institution and sale of the baronetcy, of Whig toleration and anti-absolutism, of Pitt's expansion of the peerage; and it was part of an ongoing attempt to keep the gentleman afloat, to prevent him from becoming the isolated overlord or courtier.

The English gentleman was thus able to poise himself between the world of privilege and the world of democracy. His peculiar resiliency as a model for English society was the direct result of his ability to open and close his ranks according to no fixed principle. Meanwhile, his birth and wealth generated new models—gentlemen of breeding, of education—that preserved the idea of the gentleman from any ease of definition. And it was this complex opening out of the idea that enabled the gentleman to cheat his fate: he rode out the storm of the French Revolution because he refused to become a mere aristocrat, a mere man of rank. England, like France, felt the strong pull of the aristocracy in every area of life: unlike France, however, England did not submit to the claims of the aristocracy. Before the explosion of the civil war in 1642, there were attempts to increase aristocratic power and privilege. One Thomas Bennett was fined two thousand pounds in 1637 by the Star Chamber for telling the Earl of Marlborough that he was as good a gentleman as his lordship because the Bennetts were as good as the Leys.[13] England was going toward a Richelieu style of society, but the civil war partially arrested the growth of the tendency. The absence of a caste could cause Tocqueville to reflect on the word "gentleman":

> The difference in this matter is clear from the use of one word in each language; *gentleman* and *gentilhomme* have the same origin; but gentleman in English applies to any well-educated man, regardless of birth, whereas in France gentilhomme can only be used of a noble by birth. The meaning of these two words of common derivation has been so changed by the different social climates of the peoples, that they are quite untranslatable, at least without recourse to a periphrasis. This grammatical observation is more illuminating than the longest argument. . . . the English aristocracy has a hand in everything; it is open to all; and anyone who wished to abolish it or attack it as a body, would find it very hard to define the object of his onslaught.[14]

One reason that an assault on aristocracy in England was difficult was that England's noblemen had a moderate appetite for power, certainly a more moderate appetite than the French nobility. But the question of how the English gentry avoided revolutionary confrontation with the lower classes is ultimately beyond the scope of this essay. However, it does not seem inappropriate to follow Tocqueville's lead and speak a moment about the object of onslaught.

The aristocracy and gentry were both part of the nobility—the major and minor nobility. They had interests in common and all considered themselves gentlemen. Yet, level of expenditure, life-style, and place in the hierarchy of nobility obviously made for an order that was by no means homogeneous: the duke with ten thousand a year and the private gentleman living on a few hundred had little in common in life-style. The first belonged to the great world, had a town house for the London season, perhaps more than one great country establishment. The second had a manor house, the society of those in his circumstances, perhaps a trip to Bath for the season, and no town house. Was a revolutionist to attack a squire who had often no more property and privilege than a yeoman? Was he to attack a great nobleman who perhaps provided hundreds of people with a livelihood? Who exactly was the enemy? Oppression existed, but who were its agents? With men of very different incomes, very different origins, very different life-styles all claiming the title of "gentleman," who was to be attacked? In a society increasingly dominated by wealth, a society where people were rising and falling in the ranks of gentility, it was difficult to define (as Tocqueville has suggested) who was to be overthrown. And furthermore, wealth made a larger and vaguer base of power for the upper classes. According to Tawney's Law (after R. H. Tawney) "the greater the wealth and more even its distribution in a given society, the emptier became titles of personal distinction, but the more they multiply and are striven for."[15] Wealth meant more gentlemen and more people who wanted to be gentlemen.

THE GENTLEMAN OF HONOR 3

Gentle birth and wealth did not presuppose gentle manners and breeding, but they offered a favorable precondition for certain patterns of conduct. The instinct for regulating and perfecting conduct through the agency of manners and forms may be traced to a code of behavior that lurked beneath the surface of every gentleman's actions. This code of behavior is that vaguest of all gentlemanly generalities—honor. It offers us another model—the Gentleman of Honor.

From Chaucer to the Victorians and beyond, a gentleman was supposed to be the temple in which the abstraction called "honor" dwelt; a gentleman's actions were supposed to be governed by honorable impulses. Honor has been variously defined as reputation, morality, precedence, personal attribute, and manifestation of social status. The code of honor is a gamut of possibilities ranging from extreme simplicity to baroque elaboration.[1] Jonathan Wild sums up the variable quality of the word:

> But alas! gentlemen, what pity it is that a word of such sovereign use and virtue should have so uncertain and various an application that scarce two people mean the same thing by it?[2]

Some people refer to honor and make it the property of men of virtue and honesty; Wild, however, feels this conception is too exclusive and leaves no room for Great Men—criminals and fine gentlemen.

> In what then doth the word honor consist? Why, in itself alone. A man of honor is he that is called a man of honor, and while he is so called he so remains, and no longer. Think not anything a man commits forfeits his honor. Look abroad into the world; the prig, while he flourishes is a man of honor; when in jail, at the bar, or the tree, he is so no longer.

This is honor as repute, the most straightforward acceptation. It may apply alike to thieves—"prigs"—or men of fashion. The word begins with this notion and opens out.

Honor begins with the idea of reputation because the historical origin of dueling—honor's most notable manifestation—is connected with the medieval ordeal, a test of repute. The ordeal by fire, for example, was a religious trial devised to prove the guilt or innocence of a party accused of a crime that was not an easily provable offense (i.e., adultery). God was called on to declare the verdict: if the accused was burned by walking on hot coals, he was guilty; if he emerged unharmed, he was innocent. Reputation, in other words, was reasserted through successfully undergoing the ordeal. The single combat was another form of proving repute and honor: God again judged the men in the lists. The last notable single combat was fought in 1571.[3] Meanwhile, the duel had developed at the end of the Middle Ages as the form of asserting a rather different kind of reputation. God was not called upon to make judgments in the duel. Fate decided the winner: losing a duel did not carry any social stigma; it was refusing to fight a duel—refusing to put one's life on the line for honor's sake—that made a man unworthy of the society of gentlemen.[4]

THE FINE GENTLEMAN'S HONOR

The origins of the duel are extremely complex. Its whole relationship to law and the state arises quite early in English history but is never free of vagueness and confusion. The English Court of Chivalry, according to a statute in the reign of Richard II, was empowered to deal with cases involving injuries to honor and in matters of coat armor.[5] The Court appears as a rather mysterious institution in English history simply because it does not seem to have been very powerful. It dealt in cases too delicate for the civil law—calling a gentleman a liar or a soldier a coward—but it seems to have been an advisory board rather than a powerful arm of the state. Its heraldic functions were taken over by the Herald's College at the Renaissance. And honor and the duel had no legal significance save that connected with legislation on manslaughter and homicide.

Until the reign of Henry VIII murder and manslaughter were not clearly distinguished. What emerged during the time of the Tudors was a definite tendency on the part of the crown to legislate against private acts of violence and to attempt to monopolize violence. Lawrence Stone has pointed out that dueling began to come under heavy fire in the late sixteenth and early seventeenth century because the monarchy was using the rule of law to bring the peers and gentry under the military control of the state.[6] The peers were undergoing a process of being disarmed. The result of this tendency was three centuries of legislation that attempted to bring private acts of violence into disrepute: the state was at war with the gentleman of honor and his code of the duel. James I made a proclamation against the duel and tried to discredit its prestige among the aristocracy by saying that even surgeons and butchers were taking to it.[7] Bacon as attorney general attempted to stamp out dueling. By the reign of Charles II concrete legislation against dueling began to appear: 22 and 23 Charles II—known as the Coventry Act—stated that any person convicted of lying in wait for, or wounding, another with intent to maim or disfigure, was guilty of felony.[8] The act was applied to duelists. The next piece of legislation was 9 George I—commonly called the Black Act—it made any attempt to "maliciously and willfully" shoot at another a felony.[9] "Maliciously and willfully" meant murderously, and such a charge frequently did not hold up before a magistrate. The government continued, however, to pass laws of a similar sort. George III reasserted the basic point of George I's Act—there must be intent to murder before a man can be convicted of felony.[10] George IV's reign contributed Lord Lansdowne's Act, which reiterated one hundred years of legislation on the point of murderous intent, but also added that it was an offense to shoot at anyone.[11] The 1 Victoria, c. 85 was "An Act to amend the laws relating to offenses against the person."[12] Its provisions made shooting at anyone an offense punishable by imprisonment, killing an opponent a capital offense.

This series of laws had the approval of legal commentators, moralists, and the crown: the "laws of honor" were claimed to be no excuse for taking to the field, for defying the state and the teachings of Christianity. Both Sir William Blackstone and Sir Michael Foster asserted the illegality of the duel and claimed that the law of honor was no excuse. Unfortunately, society—the society of gentlemen—had had different ideas since the Renaissance: the rule of law was demeaning, certain redresses could not be secured in a court, and suits for libel only put a price on a good name—on honor. Gentlemen fought over everything from the seduction of a sister to a verbal misunderstanding; Charles James Fox went to the field over an opponent's slip of the tongue and would accept no apologies.[13] William Makepeace Thackeray's *Barry Lyndon* reflects the extremes to which the dueling classes would go to defend honor. Lyndon narrates how his father fought a duel even though he was in the wrong.

> But like a gentleman he scorned to apologize, and Sir Huddlestone received a ball through his hat, before they engaged with the sword. I am Harry Barry's son, sir, and will act as becomes my name and quality.

The gentleman, it was felt, had the right to combat; the "churl," the "clown," and the tradesman went to law.

The conflict thus created by the opposition of the law of the land to the law of the fashionable world came to a climax in the famous trial of Lord Cardigan in 1840. Cardigan's defense attorney claimed that his client's only object was to preserve his reputation and maintain his station as a gentleman. The verdict in the case—taking no cognizance of the 1 Victoria that made shooting illegal—was not guilty: it seems that the defense proved that no one could substantiate beyond a doubt the exact first name of Cardigan's opponent. Conviction was impossible, although all the evidence indicated that Cardigan had fired. The *Times* made the following comment on the case:

What the effect on society in general must be of letting it be understood, that there is a crime that must not, or cannot, be restrained or punished, because peers and "gentlemen" think proper to commit it, while the law declares it to be a felony, we leave those to judge who know the power of example, and the aptness of the lower orders to learn evil from their betters.[14]

The House of Lords met on February 19, 1841, to discuss the verdict and the issues of legality and public morality generated by the press. Strangely enough, the peers who had acquitted Cardigan condemned dueling on moral and legal grounds. What then did the verdict mean? Or what was the spirit of the law? J. G. Millingen, a Victorian writer on dueling, formulated the great question:

Whether the act of the 1st of Victoria was framed with the intent to put an end to dueling? If so, the trial which had occurred could only be considered as a mockery of justice.[15]

The answer of course was that a travesty of justice had occurred and that gentlemanly power—guided by honor—was the force that acquiesced to the laws and broke them at the same time. The gap between law and honor is perhaps best illustrated by army law. Officers could be court-martialed for provoking a duel, "for unofficerlike and ungentlemanlike conduct in endeavoring to persuade another to be his second in a duel,"[16] and even for reproaching a man for not fighting a duel. Yet, in 1852, a physician of the Bengal Medical Department was court-martialed for conduct unbecoming an officer and a gentleman: the man in question allowed himself to be kicked in a government office by a clerk without obtaining satisfaction.[17] The officer was acquitted, but "satisfaction" was still deemed to be the right of an officer: the unwritten code of honor and the law were both pulling at the gentleman. The conflict could only be resolved by a change of societal values, a change that did in fact occur by the late 1840s: something was happening to honor.

Punch carried on a systematic attack against affairs of honor throughout the 1840s. In an 1843 cartoon called "The Satisfaction of a Gentleman," two men meet on a field as a skeleton digs a grave.[18] Other segments of middle-class opinion helped to discredit the duel. In Pickwick Papers, Dickens made mincemeat of the dueling ethos by having two grubby law clerks adopt the language of gentlemen—at the same time that they behave like ancestors of the Marx Brothers:

"I request that you'll favour me with your card, sir," said Mr. Noddy.

"I'll do nothing of the kind, sir," replied Mr. Gunter.

"Why not, sir?" inquired Mr. Noddy.

"Because you'll stick it up over your chimney piece, and delude your visitors to the false belief that a gentleman has been to see you, sir," replied Mr. Gunter.

"Sir, a friend of mine shall wait on you in the morning," said Mr. Noddy.

"Sir, I'm very much obliged to you for the caution, and I'll leave particular directions with the servants to lock up the spoons," replied Mr. Gunter.

Alfred Jingle, Esquire, that master of the put-down, is also used to discredit the ideal when he dismisses a gentleman challenger by telling him that he is drunk. In 1850, Richard Cobden threatened to hand a certain captain who challenged him over to the police. The seventh Earl of Shaftesbury acted similarly in 1854. Victorian earnestness was unwilling to make light of death. The Prince Consort was shocked by dueling and recommended courts of honor for settling questions of offense. One reaction to Prince Albert's suggestion was an emendation in the Articles of War made in 1844. It was declared to be

suitable to the character of honorable men to apologize and offer redress of wrong or insult committed, explanation and apologies for the same.[19]

But honor never attained the legal status in the Anglo-Saxon world that it did in Southern Europe. The English gentleman's honor was a private matter; it was defended in secret at dawn. Its integrity was no public concern; its violent assertion was dangerous. And by the sixties duels were definitely anachronistic. Barry Lyndon—speaking supposedly at the beginning of the nineteenth century—laments the usages that were not in fact abandoned until Thackeray was a mature man:

Sixty years ago a man was a *man*, in old Ireland, and the sword that was worn by his side was at the service of any gentleman's gizzard, upon the slightest difference. But the good old times and usages are fast fading away. One scarcely ever hears of a meeting now.

Honor, as we have noted, is not a unitary concept: its various acceptations each radiate new subtypes of the gentleman. But before continuing on to the other acceptations of the term, we will sum up honor as repute in the fashionable world.

The fine gentleman was the preeminent member of the dueling classes; his honor was a kind of secular state of grace, always liable to defilement. He is the man of fashion who mixes personal sense of worth with an equal measure of public opinion and derives a code that demands satisfaction for violations of integrity. He is concerned with the "Point of Honour," which is a term that refers to all offenses against the person as lies. These lies, however, do not shame the offender but only the offended. Jonathan Wild sums up the fashionable code: "No, it is not in the lie's going from us, but in its coming to us, our honour is injured." One does not lie to an equal, and so it is that offenses are attempts to treat one's opponent as an inferior. Status must be reasserted. If it is not, humiliation is the result—a diminishing of gentlemanly integrity. The code of the dueling classes was only operative among equals. A gentleman did not duel with a strolling player. It followed that a man not of gentlemanly status could not invoke his honor in a quarrel and could not be humiliated. Thus the very use (or abuse) of the word honor connoted gentlemanly station: at first the dueling classes were those who had inherited honor from their ancestors or derived it from their status as officers; later they came to include professionals whose sense of their own importance, whose enjoyment of occupational status in a society that required their services, entitled them to the privileges of gentlemen. And finally, honor was appropriated by the lower middle class, by clerks and shopboys who felt they were gentlemen. The last phase of honor—the period in Victorian history when it was undergoing democratization—coincided with the decline of the duel among the traditional gentlemanly class. The ultimate sanction of physical violence was a mockery in an age when jaunty office boys took to parodying the solemn ceremony of men of birth and substance.

Dickens besmirched the idea of gentlemanly honor in *Little Dorrit* by reducing it to the touchiness and bravado of a street character named Blandois, a man who felt that murderous self-assertion was the essence of being a gentleman. The last notable duel was fought in 1852. *The British Army Despatch* said that when the duel went out "the bully has an undisputed field day."[20]

HONOR AND HONESTY

Honor, while always involved with the defense of personal integrity, need not and does not stop with the code of the duel. The moral acceptation of the word generates a second kind of gentleman of honor. Honor becomes the "absence of self-reproach." A man is the only judge of his honor; his reputation is encapsulated and self-referring. This is the honor of Samuel Richardson's Sir Charles Grandison who refuses to duel with the profligate Sir Hargrave Pollexfen because he does not adhere to "vulgar notions of honour," to the usages of the dueling classes. This is the code of the Christian gentleman immune from the touchiness and obsession with forms and reputations that are the hallmarks of the fine gentleman's code. In the world of opinion, his code is found in antiduelist treatises. *The British Code of Duel: A Reference to the Laws of Honour and The Character of a Gentleman* is an anonymous, sermonizing treatment of the duel published in 1824: its "great object" is to attract attention to the character of a gentleman, a character that will often prevent duels. The author defines honor as "a principle generated by virtue, as demonstrated in useful and agreeable services to the community."[21] The gentleman is equated with the Christian, and honor becomes humanity and benevolence. The eighteenth-century fictional counterpart of this gentleman of honor is Richardson's Sir Charles: the man whose virtue is geared toward making those around him happy, whose honor is too humane to risk his life or another's in a duel. The man of honor as a Christian is an altogether different kind of gentleman from the fine gentleman as duelist. Sir Charles's declaration could have come out of the pages of an antiduelist manual: "Life I would not put upon the perhaps involuntary twitch of a finger." J. C. Bluett in *Dueling and the Laws of Honour Examined* (1835) makes Sir Charles's point: dueling and the law of honor are repugnant to both common sense and Christian charity.[22]

HONOR AND INTEGRITY

A third acceptation of the word honor is involved with middle-class integrity, self-importance, financial status, and independence of the values of the dueling classes. This "honor" is partly an extension of the landed code into the middle classes; it is the transference—but certainly not without alteration—of traditional gentlemanly values to the people

in the professions, industry, and commerce. The middle-class gentleman of honor in the world of fact is the kind of man that John Ruskin
described his father as in *Praeterita:*

> My father began business as a wine merchant, with no capital, and a
> considerable amount of debts bequeathed him by my grandfather. He
> accepted the bequest, and paid them all before he began to lay by any-
> thing for himself,—for which his best friends called him a fool, and I,
> without expressing any opinion as to his wisdom, which I knew in such
> matters to be at least equal to mine, have written over his grave that he
> was an "entirely honest merchant."

The life of the Ruskin family at Hearne Hill was one that was guided
by honor, but the honor of financial responsibility, Evangelical devotion
to duty, and class pride. Mr. Ruskin's conscientiousness and scrupulos-
ity was a way of life: he worried himself over getting orders for wine,
over meeting commitments, over "getting on." Meanwhile, Evangelical
religion set the family—perhaps eccentrically—apart from the usages
of the great world. And class pride—Mrs. Ruskin's acute, if over-
developed sense of her place in society, of her inferiority in rank to her
neighbors who delivered calling cards in their carriages—molded the
family into a self-satisfied unit that did not care to impinge directly on
any world higher than its own. The Ruskins had great respect for
rank; Mr. Ruskin's summer trips gave John a chance to see almost all
the great houses of England. The young boy characteristically *looked* at
them, but did not desire to live in splendor; he was content with being
the son of a middle-class gentleman.[23] Awe did not change to envy.
And Mr. Ruskin likewise enjoyed the role of admirer of rank without
entertaining illusions of adopting the values of persons of rank. John
captures his father's attitude perfectly when he describes the family
stays at Continental hotels. Though his father

> never went into society, he all the more enjoyed getting a glimpse, rev-
> erentially, of fashionable people—I mean, people of rank—he scorned
> fashion,—and it was a great thing for him to feel that Lord and Lady—
> were on the opposite landing, and that, at any moment, he might con-
> ceivably meet and pass them.

Disdain for fashion—for the values of the dueling class—did not pre-
clude reverence for rank; but this was reverence at a distance, reverence
that did not forget the claims of the self. Tufthunting and toadyism

were out of the question: the Ruskins had too much pride and sense of their own worth—too much sense of honor.

Another Evangelical family—the Thorntons of Battersea Rise, the ancestors of E. M. Forster—had a similar sense of independence from the aristocracy. The family integrity at the beginning of the nineteenth century centered in its City banking interest. Henry Thornton, in his descendant's words, was "public spirited" and "full of integrity." Lionel Trilling describes the social climate of the Thornton household: "Battersea Rise was not an aristocrat's home, and Henry Thornton would not have wanted it to be; he was contemptuous of his brother Robert's social aspirations and much annoyed by the breakfast party which Robert gave for Queen Charlotte and her daughters, and he regretted that his father had allowed his sister to marry Lord Leven. But Henry Thornton's house represented an idea of dignity and freedom."[24] This was the idea of middle-class honor. Noel Annan, in describing the ethos of the Evangelicals of Clapham Common and the intellectuals connected with the set, speaks of their "duty to hold themselves apart from the world given over to vanities which men of integrity rejected because they were content to labor in the vineyard where things of eternal significance grew."[25] This sense of duty coupled with a feeling of apartness from the aristocracy is certainly a hallmark of the middle-class gentleman of honor.

The middle-class man finds archetypal representation in Victorian fiction in Mrs. Craik's *John Halifax, Gentleman.* John Halifax was a beggar boy whose father was "a gentleman and a scholar"; he worked his way to respectability and reclaimed—after a series of heroic acts of public service in a small village—the title of "Gentleman." After establishing his family in a manor house and prospering as a squire and manager of the tanning factory where he rose to respectability and solvency, John encounters some difficulties with Lord Luxmore, the local magnate. John's workmen are Luxmore's tenants, and they are apparently living in squalor because of their landlord's neglect of his duty. John says he will rely "on your lordship's kindliness—your sense of honor." Luxmore offers the old reply of the dueling classes: "Honor is only spoken of between equals." The debate of the question of honor does not stop with this rebuff. Later in the novel, Lord Luxmore's son Ravenel wants to marry John's daughter Maud; this is impossible. Difference in rank is not Halifax's primary objection to the match: there are nonworldly considerations, "personal things which strike at the root of home—nay, honor." Even Luxmore's son realizes that his father's aristocratic honor is the impediment; he refers to that honor as "a foul tattered rag, fit to be torn down by an honest gust." The honest gust is the middle-class honor of Halifax. John refuses the proposed match and informs the young aristocrat that "your world is not our world, nor your aims our aims." John tells Ravenel that he (Ravenel) was born not only to be a nobleman, but a gentleman and a man made in the image of God. The novel ends with Ravenel returned from America after much suffering: he renounces his title and is thus allowed to marry Maud. He is no longer a fashionable nobleman but a gentleman of honor.

In a piece like "Mr. Brown's Letters to a Young Man About Town," Thackeray is working toward a portrait of the middle-class gentleman. Mr. Brown, in a sense, offers his nephew a series of lessons on the question of his place in society, its meaning, its duties, its limitations, its advantages. The gentleman in the middle ranks of society does not have the privileges of the man of rank and fashion. But Mr. Brown, in answering an old snob that he knew in his youth, announces a credo for the man of honor:

> I would have you know, Mr. Ruffles, that, after all, a gentleman can but be a gentleman; that though we Browns have no handles to our names, we are quite as well bred as some folks who possess these ornaments.

(Here we have echoes of Elizabeth Bennett telling Mr. Darcy that they are equal insofar as her father is a gentleman and Darcy is a gentleman.) Mr. Brown's honor inheres in his self-esteem, personal integrity, and independence of aristocratic values. And he tells his nephew the difference between a man of fashion and rank and a middle-class gentleman: "Yours is the useful part in life and theirs the splendid." But Thackeray's quintessential statement on honor is his definition of a gentleman in *The Four Georges*:

> What is it to be a gentleman? Is it to have lofty aims, to lead a pure life, to keep your honour virgin; to have the esteem of your fellow citizens, and the love of your fireside; to bear good fortune meekly; to suffer evil with constancy; and through evil or good to maintain truth always? Show me the man whose life exhibits these qualities, and him we will salute as a gentleman, whatever his rank may be; show me the prince who possesses them, and he may be sure of our love and loyalty.

To "keep your honor virgin" no longer merely means to maintain your public repute: it involves being an honest man, a man whose public reputation is high because his private conduct is above reproach. This idealization of the gentleman of honor was no late insight into the theme; Thackeray's thoughts on the middle-class gentleman had already begun to take shape by the period of *The Book of Snobs:*

> What is it to be a gentleman? Is it to be honest, to be gentle, to be generous, to be brave, to be wise, and, possessing all these qualities, to exercise them in the most graceful outward manner? Ought a gentleman to be a loyal son, a true husband, an honest father? Ought his life to be decent—his bills to be paid—his tastes to be high and elegant—his aims in life lofty and noble?

The two statements taken together offer a new man of honor. Honor as a social value is no longer obsession with dishonor, but a positive value: a gentleman of honor is not the oversensitive duelist, but the proverbial "truth-telling Englishman," the man of integrity, the man of responsibility and respectability. Honor has gone from being a matter of forms and appearances to being a matter of character.

Dickens also played a major part in prying honor apart from the code of men of birth. His novels are a veritable procession of boys and men who refuse to submit to the world's lies and sordidness and who protect their repute and integrity by decent and manly acts of self-assertion. Oliver Twist defends his mother's reputation in the workhouse by giving the bully Noah Claypole a drubbing; Nicholas Nickleby enjoys the liberating experience of beating up the brutal schoolmaster Squeers, a man who has tried to degrade him by making him a party to the school's corruption; Pip in *Great Expectations* gains stature as a man when he abandons his snobbery, shows love for a common convict, and learns that gentleness means more than pride of position. Whether through humane use of force—as opposed to swords and pistols—or through kindliness, Dickens's gentlemen aspire to a higher kind of honor than that of the man of birth.

THE GENTLEMAN OF BREEDING

4

Special qualities of life and types of behavior can leave the atmosphere of the manor house and the ancient family. For, like honor, behavior and manners cannot be confined to men of rank and blood. Behavior, in a word, is an ultimately democratic criterion for gentility that had aristocratic origins. The *Oxford English Dictionary* describes a gentleman as "A man in whom gentle birth is accompanied by appropriate qualities and behaviour; hence, in general, a man of chivalrous instincts and fine feelings." The word "hence" makes an easy transition from birth and qualities to qualities alone. While "instincts" still retains something of the notion of birth, the essence of the definition is contained in the reference cited from *The Tatler:* "The Appellation of Gentleman is never to be affixed to a Man's Circumstances but to his behaviour in them." Good blood probably sired the concept of good behavior, but the two concepts were not inseparable. They could join forces or they could go off in separate directions. But behavior is a vague term; Steele's remark in *The Tatler* indicates that he had in mind the courtesy, honesty, and liberality that the de Coverley papers assign to Sir Roger. The sentimentalized, sanitized squire was a model of good conduct. Sir Roger was fair-minded, above meanness, above moral reproach. Yet he was only one possible consequence of behavior as the test of the gentleman. For behavior is a loaded word in English usage and can take us from the ceremonious courtesies of Chaucer's knight to the stylized modishness of Lord Chesterfield. The word is a spectrum containing many possible models: their least common denominator is that they all involve a man's actions in society as a measure of his gentlemanliness.

Behavior—manners, breeding, life-style, feelings in action—is the component within the idea of the gentleman capable of the largest expansion. Our next concern is the two pervasive models in literature and history: the country boor and the man of fine breeding, the gentleman of little breeding and the fine gentleman, what Esme Wingfield-Stratford calls the lump and the leaven.[1] Both are literary types and historical models. Clearly such a discussion will involve a certain amount of labeling; yet the distinctions to be made are vital to an understanding of how the concept of manners shaped the gentlemanly ideal.

THE GENTLEMAN AS BOOR

We begin, in a sense, with the gentleman in a state of nature, with Thomas Babington Macaulay's famous (and bitterly disputed) portrait of the squirearchy at the end of the seventeenth century. The class of gentlemen described by Macaulay is characterized by its provinciality, coarseness, and ignorance; it had little to recommend it as gentlemanly but its pagan sense of honor. Macaulay writes off the squire in a few brilliant strokes:

> His ignorance and uncouthness, his low tastes and gross phrases, would, in our time, be considered as indicating a nature and breeding thoroughly plebeian. Yet he was essentially a patrician, and had, in large measure, both the virtues and vices that flourished among men set from their birth in high place, and accustomed to authority, to observance, and to self-respect. It is not easy for a generation which is accustomed to find chivalrous sentiments only in company with liberal studies and polished manners to image to itself a man with the deportment, the vocabulary, and the accent of a carter, yet punctilious on matters of genealogy and precedence, and ready to risk his life rather than see a stain cast on the honor of his house.[2]

This, of course, is history as stereotype: Macaulay may have read a dozen books to write a sentence, but he extracted the same ingredients from each of the twelve. A Whig looking for Tory squires who were uncouth, he found them in abundance. J. H. Plumb—to mention only one recent historian who has taken issue with Macaulay's generalization—has proven beyond doubt that all squires were not boors.[3] In his essay, "The Walpoles: Father and Son," he shows that country squires were often not the flat characters that Macaulay would offer us. Robert Walpole's father, a provincial in his life-style at Houghton, was nonetheless a carefully bred gentleman, a man of learning and considerable polish in his manners. Yet no amount of historical scholarship can overturn the stereotype that Macaulay has created. First of all, historians are beginning to discover (or rediscover) that many men fit the pattern. Professor Lawrence Stone reinforces, if somewhat grudgingly, Macaulay's point:

> Macaulay undoubtedly exaggerated the sluttishness of the minor rural gentry after the Restoration, but the distinction between the insular fox-hunting squire and the travelled and cultivated nobleman was one that cut deep into seventeenth and eighteenth century society.[4]

Not only does the country squire as boor cut deep into English society, but he leaves a mark so deep on literature that the lines of art and reality are blurred. The interpenetration of history and literature on the question of the squirearchy can be seen in the remark of one Elizabeth Grant, a lady visiting Nottinghamshire in the 1820s. After being introduced to Mr. Hallowes, she commented: "A regular country Squire, fit for a novel—short, chubby, good looking, shooting, fishing, hunting, hospitable, kindly, a magistrate, and not an ounce of brains!"[5] Here it appears that the only way to describe social reality is by appealing to fiction. The squire is both social reality and literary archetype.

To begin with the social reality, we find abundant corroboration of Macaulay. Esme Wingfield-Stratford speaks of "the squire original,"[6] Mr. Henry Hastings. Squire Hastings was a seventeenth-century gentleman, the fourth son of the Earl of Huntingdon. Lord Shaftesbury's portrait of him describes his hall as filled with hounds, crossbows, animal skins, and birds' nests. The squire kept a stick by his trencher to protect his meat from kittens; he stirred his tun of beer with a sprig of rosemary, and owned two books—John Foxe's *Book of Martyrs* and the Bible. His chapel was used as a larder. *The Dictionary of National Biography* calls him "the typical country squire of the time."

We can find kindred spirits right into the nineteenth century. Sir Tatton Sykes (born in 1772) "devoted all his time to agriculture, stock breeding, and fox-hunting."[7] His manners were appropriate for the taproom and the stable; his behavior was that of a yeoman rather than a gentleman. Another member of the squirearchy, George Osbaldeston, "the squire of England," was an early nineteenth-century gentleman who lived to ride to hounds and stake odds on horses. The *DNB* claims that he was incapable of "doing anything approaching an ungentlemanly action." Yet such a remark involves a definition of gentlemanly behavior that has nothing to do with honesty or good breeding. After fraudulently staking odds against his own horse by pulling him in during a trial contest, he was accused of robbery by Lord George Bentinck. While "honor" did not demand honesty in dealings, it did provoke Osbaldeston to offer Lord George a challenge. Lord George refused and Squire Osbaldeston threatened to "pull his nose" at the first opportunity at Tattersall's.[8] This ill-bred form of redress, while it has historical roots in the degradation of a knight by the king, was not considered to be a viable alternative to the duel for the gentleman in the nineteenth century; one commentator calls it the usage of "ruffians." And Mr. Wingfield-Stratford's description of Osbaldeston and his friends watching two stableboys as they cut each other with whips while riding certainly indicates that the squire's amusements were often barbaric.[9]

Ruffian or barbarian would certainly be no inappropriate term for a man like John Mytton, Esquire. This nineteenth-century squire of Halston was a "thoroughbred" according to his biographer Nimrod: he traced his pedigree to 1373 in Shrewsbury.[10] The stable imagery used in describing Mytton is fitting enough. Mytton began to ride to hounds at the age of twelve "in a red coat and cap, like Puss in Boots." He claimed he read nothing at Oxford but the *Stud Book* and *The Racing Calendar*. (Nevertheless, he did pick up some Greek before his expulsion from Westminster and Harrow.) In any event, he devoted his life to the chase and the pheasant shoot, the practical joke, and the bottle. "Nimrod" says, "The air and character of gentleman were strongly impressed on his carriage."[11] Perhaps so. But we receive our most vivid impressions of him robbing his own steward while disguised as a carter or getting drunk and putting a bear in the bed of his houseguest or setting his own shirt on fire to cure a case of the hiccoughs. Mytton was perhaps mad, but he brought the behavior of the bumpkin foxhunting gentleman to a pitch of mad perfection. He lived for physical sensation—both pleasure and pain. He tracked wildfowl in the frost dressed only in a shirt. He rode to hounds with three broken ribs. He represents the impulse of the barbarian that J. S. Mill describes in "Civilization": the ability to suffer pain as a matter of course. But like the barbarian, he was free of the manners and refinements that civilization brought. In a perfect symbolic act, he threw his wife's lapdog up to the ceiling: the pampered, domesticated animal—civilization, in a sense—provoked his wrath. So did opulence, fashion, and exclusiveness. He bragged that he had never been to Almack's: he had a sovereign contempt for the world of polished manners. Or any manners. He related to his friends instead through a series of practical jokes, through riding a bear into the drawing room. And he and his monkey enjoyed their bottle: a detail too important to bypass; for Mytton was a companion and competitor with the beasts, not a man whose behavior fitted him for society.

Literary evidence about the bumpkin squire is also abundant. In the seventeenth century George Farquhar's *The Beaux' Stratagem* presents us with Squire Sullen. A model of grossness and brutality, he is memorable for his famous line, "My head aches consumedly." Always calling for a dram and refusing to go to Church, he is contrasted with his tea-drinking, refined wife who longs for the pleasures of London society. The town-country dichotomy set up in the play also offers the contrast of Squire Sullen the sot with the fine gentleman who eventually goes off to London with Mrs. Sullen. And the squire is happy at the end of the play: finally rid of his wife, he can abandon himself to cockfighting and drinking his cup of ale; picquet, ombre, and tea are finally banished from his house. Farquhar, like Fielding in the eighteenth century, is making a statement about the insularity of certain gentlemen, about their imperviousness to culture and polished manners.

And by the eighteenth century this insular character of the gentry was reinforced by disillusionment with the Hanoverian succession. Squire Western cries out against "a parcel of Roundheads and Hannover rats"; the Court is the target of his abuse, and the "world" that his sister appeals to in matters of conduct is nothing to him. The Game Laws and the consolidation of his estate with Allworthy's are his major concern. He unites obsession with hunting and property when he brings Sophia and Tom together: "Western . . . burst into the room, and with his hunting voice and phrase cried out, 'To her boy, to her, go to her.'" The imagery of the chase was the only means that Western had for describing the marital union.

But perhaps the coarsest, most unmannerly squire in English literature is Thackeray's Sir Pitt Crawley. Becky Sharp goes into his service with high hopes: "At least, I shall be amongst *gentle folks,* and not vulgar City people." Yet she is greeted by

> a man in drab breeches and gaiters, with a dirty old coat, a foul old neck cloth lashed around his bristly neck, a shining bald head, a leering red face, a pair of winkling grey eyes, and a mouth perpetually on the grin.

Becky asks for Sir Pitt, and this old man answers that he is the baronet and expects to be tipped for carrying her baggage. He speaks in "the coarsest and vulgarest Hampshire accent." Writing to Amelia, Becky sums him up:

> Fancy an old, stumpy, short, vulgar, and very dirty man, in old clothes and shabby old gaiters, who smokes a horrid pipe, and cooks his own horrid supper in a saucepan. He speaks with a country accent, and swore

a great deal at the old charwoman, at the hackney coachman who drove us to the inn where the coach went from, and on which I made the journey outside *for the greater part of the way.*

Sir Pitt is a gentleman by birth and wealth, but his claim to the title stops there. His behavior and life-style are those of a crafty steward: Thackeray makes much of the fact that Queen's Crawley is a property to be exploited and nothing more to Sir Pitt.

THE GENTLEMAN AND ETIQUETTE

The ill-breeding, coarseness, provinciality, and disregard for manners never went unchallenged. From William of Wykeham who said that "manners maketh man" to Lord Chesterfield and the Victorians, the "literature of courtesy" has offered constant opposition to grossness and vulgarity. Since courtesy literature offers the "social standards of an age"[12] (and changes from age to age), and since it concerns everything from eating a dinner to ruling a kingdom, the following discussion will limit itself to the fine gentleman in the eighteenth and nineteenth century, to the man of fine manners who is the social opposite of the boor. We will enlist Chesterfield and one of his predecessors along with a nineteenth-century courtesy writer to get a sense of the range contained in an expression like good behavior.

Before turning to courtesy writers, however, we should have some idea of the general concepts we are dealing with: courtesy and etiquette. Courtesy, according to J. E. Mason, is "a code of ethics, esthetics, or peculiar information for any class conscious group."[13] The word is bound up with a sense of belonging to a group; it is at the same time a code; it binds only members of a certain group. Etiquette is a word that originally denoted a ticket to label bags so that their contents would not be challenged. Later, there were rules of etiquette printed on tickets.[14] The rules of etiquette thus relate to a method of defense; they are in use to meet challenges or encroachments. Or, as the author of *Hints on Etiquette and the Usages of Society* (1861) puts it, etiquette is a barrier where the law leaves off.[15] Taken together, courtesy and etiquette give us a sense of what behavior means in terms of gentility: it is an assertion of membership in a group and a barrier to incursion by outsiders. Conduct determines gentility; where behavior is unacceptable, the courtesy writer can deny the gentility of the person in question. Behavior opens a whole new hierarchy: an exclusiveness based on manners.

Lord Chesterfield's *Letters to His Son* offers the free admission that "good company" does not consist solely of people of the first quality. There are other, more important considerations than blood. His vision of the man of the world, the man of fine breeding, was the man of easy carriage, polished manners, adeptness, well-tempered knowledge. For preeminence in society, Chesterfield emphasized the qualities of the fine gentleman, not the blood of the noblest house. Chesterfield's fine gentleman brought to the highest pitch of perfection the values of the courtier, man of the world, man of pleasure: he was a lineal descendant of Castiglione's perfect courtier, a man whose stage was society and whose occupation was the art of pleasing. Chesterfield seemingly adapts Castiglione's *sprezzatura*—the ease and nonchalance of the courtier in every social situation—and tries to make his clumsy bastard son into the unlabored, graceful, appealing man of fashion. Chesterfield's letters are a brilliant attempt at character formation, perhaps one of the most interesting practical documents in the history of dissimulation and social manipulation. Castiglione recommended that his courtier avoid "the smell of the midnight oil"—the appearance of effort and stress. Chesterfield rigidified this graceful falsehood into a code of counterfeit actions calculated to make a man "shine." His chief social assumption was that gentle birth could not answer for lack of good breeding and good sense; he was, even though he rejected the role, a reformer of sorts. Macaulay's country boors were the object of his disdain, and he warned his godson to shun those "rustic, illiberal sports of guns, dogs, and horses, which characterize our English Bumpkin country squires." [16] Not only did he find the sporting gentleman illiberal, but he also condemned pedants and egoists, men who betrayed their lack of gentlemanliness by labored behavior. Ease and civility were the cardinal virtues and their consequences in the great world were immediate social acceptance and the opportunity to play a central role, to be a courtier. Young Philip Stanhope did become an MP and foreign envoy, but his gracelessness, stuttering, and lack of "parts" prevented him from attaining diplomatic distinction. This young man bred for the great world was a failure: despite the coaching of tutors and the innumerable lectures on rational pleasures and sacrificing to the "Graces," the boy was an imperfect product. He somehow could not be shaped for success in the great world.

Chesterfield's legacy goes beyond his practical failure; the fine gentleman that he delineated with such care was behind the reality of a Brummell, sired (Chesterfield would have died to think) innumerable bucks and bloods and swells in fiction like Bulwer-Lytton's Pelham, was parodied by the out-at-the-elbows Victorian gent, and partially sat for every unflattering portrait of the gentleman in Victorian literature. And besides his influence on literature and society, he left a blueprint for social action that became part of the stock and trade of every courtesy writer. "Endeavor, as much as you can, to keep company with people above you."[17] The fashionable dicta thrown out in the course of his relationship with Philip form a model code of behavior. Talk not too often, tell stories seldom, never hold anyone by the button, take rather than give the tone of the company, avoid argumentative conversations, avoid speaking of yourself, be on your guard. The Chesterfieldian fine gentleman, in a sense, could be (and was in later courtesy books) reduced to a series of catch phrases.[18] At worst, he could be seen as a series of epigrams programmed into the elegant deportment of a nonentity. And yet, the Chesterfieldian fine gentleman was something more: he was penetrating, self-contained, and judicious. He had the sense to "seem to take the world as it is." But he had the know-how to turn it to his own devices. He was too smart to be a rake, too shrewd not to feign religious sentiment. And most of all, he was too much of a gentleman—too aware of the world's usages and their claims on the self—ever to forget courtesy and civility. "Give Dayrolles a chair" were supposedly Chesterfield's last words: everyone must be accommodated; the great world must be frictionless.

Johnson's well-known, savage appraisal of the letters was part of an ongoing response to everything the fine gentleman stood for. He said Chesterfield taught "the morals of a whore and the manners of a dancing master."[19] The fine gentleman was the culmination of a fashionable tradition that had easily recognizable roots in the Restoration Man of Mode: Sir Fopling Flutter in Sir George Etherege's comedy is a ridiculous but direct forebear of the fine gentleman. "A complete gentleman . . . ought to dress well, dance well, fence well, have a genius for love letters, an agreeable voice for a chamber, be very amorous, something discreet but not overconstant." Chesterfield would have objected to this trivial reduction of his code of behavior: he thought dancing a minor accomplishment and one that could easily be overemphasized. But the fact remains that to be *amiable* in the Chesterfieldian sense was to be the agreeable, stylized, frenchified fine gentleman who ran perilously close to foppery.

But perhaps the most telling indictment of Chesterfield is the shallowness of his intellectual ancestors in the medium of the courtesy book, the social ethos of those who shared his values. Chesterfield wrote after a writer like Colonel James Forrester, author of *The Polite Philosopher: Or The Art Which Makes a Man Happy and Agreeable to Others* (1734). Yet, Forrester's book seems like a travesty of Chesterfieldian values. It begins with the author's intent to make vice ridiculous; yet it will not talk about sins, but about "impoliteness." The "polite philosopher"— disclaiming the role of pedagogue—speaks of reason, calmness, and good nature as the cardinal points of a polite character. "Without Reason there is no being a fine gentleman":[20] it is, the author says, like a fop's waistcoat; it should be worn out of sight. Here, of course, we have an anticipation of Chesterfield's remarks on learning: that it should be used deftly and not flaunted. "Calmness" is again Chesterfieldian: it involves Chesterfield's disdain for violent emotions, his belief that a gentleman should smile, but never laugh. "Good Nature" maintains that "disquiet is the greatest evil." The smoothness of social intercourse that Chesterfield values is reduced to what seems to us like a parody. Chesterfield and Forrester each make the same point about religion: mockery of belief is grossly impolite. Forrester begins his treatment of religion by saying that the subject is perhaps "too gauche to mention": this is the mincing evasiveness of much courtesy literature that deals with the fine gentleman. Forrester is too polite to confront any issue; he reminds us more than once that he will not be too serious for fear of offending the beau monde with gravity. Courtesy literature—by its very nature a literature bound by a code and concerned with defense— even defends itself from its readers: Forrester's language is so polite and evasive and unemphatic that it rarely declares anything but the necessity to avoid giving offense. (Forrester urges his readers to be "complacent," not "vehement": any kind of passion or commitment ruffles "the sweetest of features.") The manual ends by talking about "Good Humour" and recommends the habit of being pleased to the fine gentleman. Taken in conjunction with the other forms of evading unpleasantness, this amounts to enjoining the fine gentleman to limit himself to a life of pleasing and being pleased, to an existence that takes as its purpose the art of being smug.

Unfortunately, Chesterfield himself cannot be freed from this charge of complacency. For all his greatness, his concern is what Cardinal Newman referred to as setting "the surface of things right."[21] The fine gentleman attempted to quell conflict, to please and be pleased, to use dissimulaton and evasion in the interests of surface harmony. This surface harmony—this attempt on the part of Chesterfield to make society into an association of complacent persons—is classically described by Newman. The often-quoted (and more often-misunderstood) passage in *The Idea of a University* is an ironic definition of the gentleman, an attempt to sum up the social techniques and modes of behavior that the fine gentleman uses to assure tranquil social intercourse. Most of all, the gentleman does not inflict pain, and therefore does not engage in controversy. His object is harmony, and to achieve it he will acquiesce to what he does not believe, be silent rather than cause argument, be completely without a selfhood in the interests of his company.

ETIQUETTE AND AGGRESSION

But social harmony as an ideal of courtesy writers became difficult to maintain by the nineteenth century. Chesterfield recommended that his son endeavor to associate with people above him: this was not a difficult task for an earl's son; the scions of the major nobility accepted each other as equals. G. O. Trevelyan informs us of the ease with which the aristocracy and greater gentry interacted in the eighteenth century: everybody knew everybody else.[22] The society that Chesterfield wrote about was essentially the society of men of birth, rank, and wealth. By the nineteenth century the definition of "good company" had changed considerably; the nineteenth-century courtesy writer was focusing on a different segment of society: the middle classes, what the eighteenth century called the "middling sort" of people. These people—the servant-keeping classes—had social aspirations and were attempting to close the gap between themselves and the old gentry. And they were attempting to alter their life-style to conform to that of the gentry. "There is certainly evidence to show that the modest gentleman and the prosperous merchant, the better-paid clergy and the professional, lived not only comfortably but with some refinement."[23] Besides their life-style, their manners were a means of closing the gap: they aped the behavior and deportment of the "quality." And it was the courtesy book that took particular cognizance of their aspiring position; courtesy writers understood their audiences and understood the obstacles in the way of social mobility. By the nineteenth century the courtesy writer's task was to try to integrate these new people into the old framework through teaching them how to behave. One writer—a "Lady of Rank" in 1861—

sums up her object: "If these 'hints' save the blush upon *one cheek*, or smooth the path into 'society' of only *one* honest family, the object of the author will be attained."[24] The manual is intended for those imperfectly acquainted with how to handle new wealth; its object is to prevent "mortification"—the greatest disharmony of all in social intercourse. And its underlying assumption is that behavior in society must be defensive:

> Not that you may *care* the more for strangers by showing them civility, but you should scrupulously avoid the imputation of being deficient in good breeding; and if you do not choose to be polite for *their* sakes, you ought to be so for your own.[25]

The author might have added, "in order that you may maintain your own improved position."

The competition for a place in good society was tremendous. Our "Lady of Rank" continues:

> The English are the most aristocratic people in the world; always endeavoring to squeeze through the portals of rank and fashion, and then slamming the door in the face of any unfortunate devil who may happen to be behind them.[26]

Here we are in a different social world from that of Chesterfield's letters; in Chesterfield the conflict in society was hidden by the good manners of all those concerned; our "Lady of Rank"—only some ninety years later—has presented us with an unadorned image of exclusion. The pushing and shoving of middle-class people to get into society was not a concern of Chesterfield or his predecessor Forrester.

But by the Regency behavior had become a form of open warfare: a man went into society in order to defend his own position and subdue pretenders to gentility. "Exclusiveness" as a term became popular during the first quarter of the nineteenth century; the weapon in this conception of society was "the cut." In an industrial age when new people were likely to be intruding on men of blood, defenses were necessary. Or as one writer put it: "In modern civilized life as it is the cut is a great institution."[27] Our Victorian "Lady of Rank" felt that it should only be used on those whose conduct had been reprehensible. Nevertheless, she is quite willing to tell how it is done: a cold bow is usually adequate.

An increased observance of ceremony is, however, the most delicate way of withdrawing from an acquaintance; and the person so treated must be obtuse, indeed, who does not take the hint.[28]

Sometimes the expression of hostility takes the form of pseudophilosophizing about the demands of a complex society: in Dickens's *Little Dorrit,* Mrs. Merdle, an odious rich woman, attempts to degrade Fanny Dorrit, an equally odious intruder from a questionable family. Mrs. Merdle rejects Fanny as a daughter-in-law (and her family too) and points out

> the impossibility of the society in which we moved, recognizing the society in which she moved—though charming, I have no doubt; the immense disadvantage at which she would consequently place the family that she had so high an opinion of, upon which we should find ourselves compelled to look down with contempt, and from which (socially speaking) we should feel obliged to recoil with abhorrence.

Mrs. Merdle takes real pleasure in saying that "Society oppresses and dominates us"—she has a radically different view of genteel life from that of the secure and totally complacent people of birth.

But perhaps the best way to offer a sustained picture of this conflict—this jostling of old and new people—is to turn to a novelist like Tobias George Smollett, a writer whose prose early registered the fact that the battle was on in the world of fashion, that the whole notion of good company was changing, that new forms of conduct were finding their way into good society. *Humphry Clinker* presents a view of this new society; it represents characters who have differing views of the condition of society, the fate of gentility, and the role of manners. The scene is Bath and Squire Bramble is nauseated by the social fluidity of this watering place. "Every upstart of fortune" comes to Bath—plunderers and usurers, plantation owners and speculators.

> Men of low birth and no breeding, have found themselves suddenly translated into a state of affluence unknown to former ages; and no wonder that their brains should be intoxicated with pride, vanity, presumption. Knowing no other criterion of greatness, but the ostentation of wealth they discharge their affluence without taste or conduct, through every channel of the most absurd extravagance; and all of them hurry to Bath, because there, without any further qualification, they can mingle with the princes and nobles of the land. Even the wives and daugh-

ters of low tradesmen, who, like shovel-nosed sharks, prey upon the
blubber of those uncouth whales of fortune, are infected with the same
rage of displaying their importance; and the slightest indisposition serves
them for a pretext to insist upon being conveyed to Bath, where they
may hobble country dances and cotillions among lordlings, squires,
counsellors, and clergy. These delicate creatures from Bedfordbury,
Butchers-Row, Crutched-friers, and Botolph-lane, cannot breathe in the
gross air of the Lower Town, or conform to the vulgar rules of a common lodging-house; the husband, therefore, must provide an entire house,
or elegant apartments in the new buildings. Such is the composition of
what is called the fashionable company at Bath; where a very inconsid-
erable proportion of genteel people are lost in a mob of impudent plebeians, who have neither understanding nor judgment, nor the least idea
of propriety and decorum; and seem to enjoy nothing so much as the
opportunity of insulting their betters.

Squire Bramble is seemingly trying to arrest the breakdown of social
distinctions, to restore the old world, but these people have made it
into the fashionable world and made that world anything but quiet
and harmonious.

In short, there is no distinction or subordination left—The different
departments of life are jumbled together—The hodcarrier, the low me-
chanic, the tapster, the publican, the shopkeeper, the pettyfogger, the
citizen, the courtier, *all tred upon the Kibes of one Another:* actuated by
the demons of profligacy and licentiousness, they are seen everywhere
rambling, riding, rolling, rushing, jostling, mixing, bouncing, cracking,
and crashing in one vile ferment of stupidity and corruption—All is
tumult and hurry; one would imagine they were compelled by some
disorder of the brain, that will not suffer them to be at rest.

The squire's nephew Jery Melford sees social collision in the fashionable world of Bath not as an anarchic but as a leavening influence:
"Those plebeians who discovered such eagerness to imitate the dress and
equipage of their superiors, would likewise, in time, adopt their maxims and their manners, be polished by their conversation, and refined
by their example." Dorothy Marshall points out that the spa was a
learning center for the middle classes; it helped to spread the conventions of "polite society" to a wider circle.[29]

Humphry Clinker actually contains several possibilities for gentlemanly models: on the one hand, Squire Bramble maintains the primacy

of the country gentleman, the man of birth: on the other hand, Jery opens the door a little wider, admits that society is a school of behavior and that its graduates can be integrated into the old social framework. Jery's tests of gentility are vaguer, more modern; the strolling actor Wilson becomes involved with Jery's sister, and Jery all but fights a duel with him:

> As his behavior was remarkably spirited, I admitted him to the privilege of a gentleman, and something would have happened had we not been prevented.

The law steps in and Wilson is reminded of his presumption in proceeding "to such extremities with the gentleman of family and fortune." The strolling actor is threatened with the Vagrant Act. Society was receptive to new people only insofar as they had substantial credit standings and respectable occupations. It was forever slamming the door or opening it a bit to let someone squeeze in.

Smollett, however, offers one vision of gentility that uses honesty and independence as its tests—Lismahago, the Scottish naval officer who in all his grotesque comicality contains traits that anticipate Thackeray's Victorian gentleman.

> I am a gentleman; and entered the service as other gentlemen do, with such hopes and sentiments as honorable ambition inspires—If I have not been lucky in the lottery of life, so neither do I think myself unfortunate—I owe no man a farthing; I can always command a clean shirt; a mutton chop, and a truss of straw; and when I die, I shall leave effects sufficient to defray the expenses of my burial.

Here we have gentlemanly integrity purged of all its arrogance, minus the trappings of fashion, devoid of an exalted sense of self-importance. Lismahago is an embryonic Dobbin: a man whose honorable behavior is not compromised by gracelessness and lack of fashionable credentials. He is the true man of breeding; but to describe him we need only recall the idealized middle-class gentleman of honor.

Finally, we can separate out three forms of behavior that characterize the gentleman in life and literature: coarse behavior, fine behavior, and honest behavior; ill manners, polished manners, simple manners. Ill manners led to barbarism; polished manners helped breed a code that led to both complacency and combativeness; simple manners led to the idealized gentleman of Christian behavior.

THE GENTLEMAN OF RELIGION 5

By the end of the eighteenth century the idea of the gentleman began to open up in contradictory ways. It expanded in different directions. Money, fashion, and manners had been added to the initial tests of birth and land. Meanwhile, religion was taking hold of the gentlemanly ideal. Macaulay's portrait of England in 1685 certainly indicates that men with little religion enjoyed the status and privilege of gentlemen. Pagan barbarism did not diminish a high sense of honor and a clear social status. Yet, within a hundred years of the period Macaulay describes, gentlemanly attitudes toward religion were beginning to change. By Victorian times they had changed so radically that the Duke of Wellington felt it was necessary to attend church services with his tenantry.

Religion was a behavioral guideline that began as a negligible influence and worked its way through the eighteenth century into a position of centrality within the idea of the gentleman. In 1739, *The Gentleman's Magazine* published a parody of the Ten Commandments supposedly written by the governing classes. The Sixth Commandment was

> miserably perverted by a set of cowardly, low-spirited, superstitious expositors who make it criminal even in men of spirit and Quality to do justice to themselves and their characters by punishing the ill manners of any little dirty Poltroon that shall assume to affront them by running him through the body, beating out his brains or any other ways and means as have in all ages been thought reasonable and reputable to secure the Regard due to their Rank and Fortune and chastise the insolence of their inferiors.[1]

Gentlemen, it is claimed, were trying to rewrite the Ten Commandments and make them into a weapon for the preservation of a deference society. The Ninth Commandment, we find, was not to extend to "Court Favorites, Royal Minions, First Ministers, Secretaries of State,

Privy Counsellors, Decypherers, Spys, Pimps, and Informers." The upper classes and their favorites were to be exempt from morality. While gentlemanly pleasure was undergoing a process of refinement—a process by which crude pleasures were gradually refined off the face of fashionable society throughout the century—there was no basic change in the fine gentleman's attitude toward vice. Chesterfield cleaned up the man of the world and offered an ideal that tolerated vice freed of its grossness; he set the surface right, made pleasure reasonable and decent.[2] Nevertheless, the surface belied the pagan ethos that was the code of the fine gentleman. The wholesale generalization of *The Encyclopedia of the Social Sciences* applies in large measure to men of fashion and privilege in the eighteenth century: "In general the plain man distinguishes morality from immorality; the gentleman distinguishes immorality from scandal."[3] Chesterfieldian ethics—summing up religious and moral duties as "exceedingly plain and simple" as worthy of only a half sentence in a letter—belonged to a combative pagan code that did not recognize altruism, abnegation, humility. And thus it is not surprising to find late seventeenth- and eighteenth-century country gentlemen who had little respect for the parson; this attitude was often shared by the fine gentleman as well. Parson Adams is a nobody—powerless in the world of gentlefolks in *Joseph Andrews*. And Macaulay records that the local curate of the late seventeenth century did not enjoy gentlemanly status: he "was not asked into the parlors of the great, but was left to drink and smoke with grooms and butlers." The important members of the clergy had the reputation for being what Newman later called "high and dry"—high on privilege, dry on spirituality.

This brings us to the relation between the Church and the gentleman in the eighteenth century. The Church was what Élie Halévy called "a branch of the aristocracy."[4] The king was its head, and the realm contained subjects of various estates: archbishops, bishops, vicars, and curates. This hierarchical gradation was just not a series of spiritual roles but a system of privilege. Livings in the Church were disposed of by the landed gentry. "Thus did the ecclesiastical constitution of the country harmonize with the political."[5] At least half of the benefices were at the disposal of the squires; others were actually sold by public auction. The result was that the Church became a place for buying and selling, parlaying interests, and jockeying for position and preferment. A right to a good living meant a man might be the vicar of a parish with a sizable income; by hiring a curate he could often secure for himself an income of a thousand pounds and pay his curate fifty pounds, Halévy cites one instance of a curate who was paid a shilling a day, the salary of a poor workman. Thus it was that some clergymen could live as gentlemen—freed from the onerous tasks of the parson. A good living in Suffolk made one rector's life easy:

> Here he became a great favorite with the country gentlemen, by whom his society was much sought; for he kept an excellent hunter, rode well up to the hounds, drank very hard. He sang an excellent song, danced remarkably well, so that the young ladies considered no party complete without him.[6]

Meanwhile, the poor curates were turning to weaving and other illiberal pursuits to earn their bread. Peter Laslett's notion of subsumption certainly describes the Church: nowhere else in English society could a better example be found of one group "living" for another.[7]

The Evangelical segment within the Church offered a strong challenge to the laxity of the clergy. By the end of the eighteenth century, nonresidence was coming under heavy fire. The Evangelicals later tried to enact laws that would set aside a fixed portion of a living for the curates. Both attempts at reform failed. Yet the Evangelicals—a party, as Halévy has put it, of emotion and action[8]—offered the idea of the gentleman a mandate for reform. In 1794, Isaac Milner said, "The great and high have forgotten that they have souls."[9] Evangelicism was one force that reminded the gentleman that he had a duty—as clergyman, as squire, as man of business—to do more than enjoy the privileges of his station. One Evangelical pamphlet written in 1801 sought to expel Parson Doolittle and Parson Merryman and replace them with Parson Lovegood.[10] This impulse toward morality was a force that the gentleman could not avoid in life and in literature.

A key model of gentlemanly morality in eighteenth-century literature is Richardson's Sir Charles Grandison—a man committed to moral reform even before the rise of Evangelicism. Sir Charles—patronizingly called a "simple English gentleman" by a haughty Italian nobleman—is the gentleman as "A GOOD MAN." Spurning pride of ancestry and fashion, he lives "to my own heart"—according to conscience. His conscience causes him to undertake the task of teaching and reforming the immoral men in his acquaintance. His cousin, Mr. Grandison—a rake who has ruined several women—is rehabilitated by Sir Charles, helped to appear "as a gentleman" by changing his life. Sir Charles saves his would-be fiancée's brother from moral and physical ruin. And he attempts, as we have noted, to reform the fine gentleman's code of honor. His works of goodness are overwhelming: the other characters in the novel seem to exist to testify to his moral superiority. If he were Catholic, the Bolognese marchioness who was to be his mother-in-law comments, he would be worthy of canonization. But his Protestantism is a central issue in the novel: he is the man of principle who cannot abandon his faith to marry a Catholic noblewoman. His strong religious conviction makes him what Harriet Byron, his future wife, calls "The Christian: the hero: the friend." And his simple manners make him "the truly fine gentleman." Guided by gentleness and forgiveness, his actions shame even his servants into reform.

The impulse to effect a moral rejuvenation of the gentleman was also manifested in nonfiction. In 1782, Vicesimus Knox, a writer on educational questions, wrote an essay called "Hints to Those Who Are Designed for the Life of a Gentleman without a Profession." The piece enjoins the gentleman to avoid idleness, to drop the stance of a man of fashion, to be useful.

> The world abounds with evil, moral, natural, real and imaginary. He alone who does all he can, wherever his influence extends, to mitigate and remove it, is the *true gentleman*. Others are only esquires, knights, baronets, barons, viscounts, earls, marquises, dukes, and kings.[11]

This bald generalization, in all its uninspired sententiousness, is a marker in the idea of the gentleman: it uses the morality of usefulness to undercut the concept of rank; it cuts the word gentleman off from the mooring of social status; it offers preeminence to men who wage God's war. Knox's remark is an example of the endless discussions about the lack of gentlemanliness of peers. It gives us an insight into why the Duke of Wellington valued the title of English gentleman above all other designations. For the gentleman was also the man who did right. The obvious consequences of the idea were recognized by Knox himself in his essay "On the Merit of Illustrious Birth": birth was no guarantee of nobility. There were many noblemen, "according to the genuine idea of nobility,"[12] who could be found at the loom, at the plow, in the shop. This is one step from the "kind hearts are more than coronets" phase of the idea of the gentleman. Victorian England would not only expand and elaborate such a theory of nobility, it would make it a starting point for imaginative speculation and test it on reality itself. The democratizing tendency of morality as a test of gentility was open to every form of perversion, distortion, and limitation that ingenuity could devise. Just as the test of manners made nice distinctions that excluded many from the pale of gentility, so also did goodness pick and choose its gentlemen.[13]

One of the first explicit, emphatic Victorian declarations about the gentleness of the ungenteel, the possibility of gentlemanliness without blood and wealth, was contained in Francis Lieber's *The Character of a Gentleman* (1846). The work devotes itself to considering the "highest" acceptation of the word gentleman.

> I believe it signifies that character which is distinguished by strict honour, self-possession, forbearance, generous as well as refined feelings and polished deportment,—a character to which all meanness, explosive irascibility and peevish fretfulness are alien; to which consequently, veracity, courage, both moral and physical, dignity, self-respect, a studious avoidance of offending others, and a liberality are habitual and have become natural.[14]

This acceptation certainly opens the door to democratization of the idea of the gentleman. Gentle qualities and gentle behavior make the gentleman. The reader may at first be disturbed by the expression "polished deportment": Lieber, however, opens even this criterion to men of simple origins. "Polish" is usually associated with high breeding, but "nevertheless may result from native qualities so strong that subsequent cultivation may become comparatively unimportant."[15] The "native qualities" are the key point. While rhapsodizing on this theme of gentility for the ungenteel, he becomes so carried away that he refers to a black slave who was a gentleman "in his humble sphere."[16] (The poor slave probably would have preferred plain freedom to genteel fantasy.) But despite our distaste for this kind of thing, we are forced to recognize the tendencies present in Lieber's remarks. The author urges his reader to "permeate your soul by a truly gentlemanly spirit."[17] Clearly this is an enterprise that can be taken on by any man.

The idea of the gentleman put forward by Sir A. Edmonstone in his *Christian Gentleman's Daily Walk* (1850) goes even further in its claims: Edmonstone feels that true gentlemanliness and true Christian behavior are wholly consonant; the growth and development of the gentleman and the growth of the Christian soul are one and the same. Edmonstone's ideal gentleman lives amid conflict and sorrow; by some "alchemy" he has the power to extract goodness from the fallen world around him. Edmonstone writes that "in his breast is deposited a Divine light, like the lamp forever burning in an Eastern shrine, which illuminates his path and directs his steps amid the perplexing shadows of a benighted world."[18] At the very least, this gentleman is veering perilously close to the territory of the saint. We should remember, however, that Edmonstone's treatment of an outstanding example of humanity insists on using the word "gentleman." When the idea of the gentleman is so democratized and spiritualized that it is difficult to identify and talk about, we cannot help but suggest that men like Edmonstone have contributed to the discrediting of the word in our own time. As more and more spiritual territory is claimed for the gentleman, he becomes almost impossible to analyze; he is everywhere and nowhere. And when claims are made for him—when we read the extravagant, idealizing, fancy prose of believers in the gentleman as good man—they often begin to sound rather flat. In short, overkill has made the gentleman into an often tedious embodiment of goodness.

In the fictional realm, Dickens was one of the most active novelists in the campaign to explode the traditional conception of the gentleman and replace it with a nebulous, spiritualized ideal. His late novels are especially rich in contrasts between the gentle and the genteel: the former emerge as paragons of virtue—dutiful, kind, loving, loyal; at times they seem all but ready for beatification. They have generally been ravaged by the genteel world of consumption and class relations and emerge with an aura of kindness and Christian selflessness. In *Great Expectations* Pip, the once snobbish young protagonist, and Magwitch, his convict benefactor, are tragically tested and broken: Pip winds up without a shred of illusion about the value of being a fine gentleman; Magwitch, the victim of the court system and its injustices toward nongentlemen, is condemned to death for wanting to see his young gentleman prosper. But Dickens makes sure that we see Magwitch as Pip's protector and large-hearted, honest friend. The qualities he is invested with by Pip make him sound like one of the courtesy writers' true gentlemen—"a man who had meant to be my benefactor, and who had felt affectionately, gratefully, and generously towards me, with great constancy through a series of years." The effect of such a gentle friend on Pip is almost immediate—he turns his life around and begins to work and live an upright existence. Dickens has also offered another example of nongenteel gentleness, Joe Gargery. As Pip's old friend from his days as a poor village boy, Joe is a lower-class embodiment of fine feeling, a distillation of ideal gentlemanly virtue in the person of a rough blacksmith. Dickens refers to him as "a gentle Christian man": the placement of the word Christian is Dickens's way of continuing the debate on what a gentleman is and at the same time expanding the conception in such a way as to detach the true gentle man from the gentleman. Joe Gargery, Pip's friend in adversity, is an open, frank, and kind man who takes his place in a whole new hierarchy: the hierarchy of human feelings as opposed to that of family, wealth, and gentle breeding. Joe also represents the direction of the English novel in the next hundred years—a turning away from the concerns of status, class, and position and a focusing on the realms of intimacy and emotion. The preeminent man or woman in the modern novel will be the person who enters most freely and authentically into the world of feelings.

Dickens finished off his treatment of the gentle man in *Our Mutual Friend,* his last major novel. The book is involved with one of his central problems—the relationships between the wellborn and the humble. After resolving a number of conflicts by having a gentleman, Eugene Wrayburn, marry a lower-class girl, Lizzy Hexam, Dickens brings together a number of well-to-do people to talk about the shocking event and give voice to the opinions of society.

> The question before the Committee is, whether a young man of very fair family, good appearance, and some talent, makes a fool or wise man of himself in marrying a female waterman, turned factory girl.

The snobs and commercial types look at the question as so much lost status and business mismanagement. But a withered little old gentleman named Twemlow, a holdover from the Regency days who wears a "first gentleman of Europe collar" and has the quiet manners of a true courteous gentleman, voices an opinion that jars the group: "I am disposed to think this is a question of the feelings of a gentleman"— "feelings of gratitude, respect, admiration, and affection." (A brief look at Dickens's description of Magwitch's attitude toward Pip will indicate that this remark matches up with the earlier one.) Twemlow's further comments reveal his position even more clearly:

I think he is the greater gentleman for the action, and makes her the greater lady. I beg to say, that when I use the word gentleman, I use it in the sense in which the degree may be attained by any man. The feelings of a gentleman I hold sacred and I confess I am not comfortable when they are made the subject of sport or general discussion.

When the phrase "attained by any man" is wedged into the idea of the gentleman, something has happened to an ancient English conception: the relatively clear and intelligible ideas about status and life-style have been dissolved forever. Without claiming that this wedge destroyed the ideal in Dickens's time, we can nevertheless identify it and link it to the rise of a nontraditional sensibility that dominated the literature and life of our own century.

THE GENTLEMAN OF EDUCATION

6

The gentleman of religion or morality, however, takes us only part of the way toward an understanding of the acceptations of the word "gentleman." The gentleman of education played a complex role in defining gentility. Never a constant in the making of a gentleman, education did not have an easily assignable place.

Modern educational theory and practice must be seen against the background of training that was offered to the sons of the aristocracy through the Renaissance. A squire's education in the Middle Ages was a very different thing from that of a clerk and university man. Education as we understand it—schools, colleges, and universities; courses of study and scholarly disciplines—was principally the province of monks and priests. The student body of the universities up to the Renaissance contained for the most part those planning to take orders.[1] The man apprenticing for knighthood—the squire—was usually boarded out in the household of a nobleman where he learned the graces, skills, and usages of his class. As late as the sixteenth century a diplomat like Richard Pace could write the following: "It becomes the sons of gentlemen to blow a horn nicely, to hunt skillfully, and elegantly to train and carry a hawk."[2] Pace claims that the study of letters was for "beggars and rustics." This view was already somewhat anachronistic, however. For by the sixteenth century the aristocracy began to appear on the books of the universities in swarms.[3] During the Tudor period the majority of the university students were not "gentlemen," but the balance was shifting from the time when aristocrats and men of ancestry were rare. J. H. Hexter describes the balance: "For every five men matriculating there as *filii plebei,* three described themselves as gentlemen's sons."[4] By the beginning of the seventeenth century Hexter maintains that the balance had even shifted further: there were six gentlemen to five plebeians. The universities were accommodating more gentlemen's sons for several reasons: decline in warfare as a gentleman's occupation, changing ideals of what a gentleman should be, and increasingly complex government and diplomatic posts that required training.

When a gentleman could no longer be a knight, when warfare could no longer be a way of life, other areas of activity had to be turned to. Public service, law, parliament, all required literate men. The schools and universities began to be places where gentlemen were prepared for what Raymond Williams calls "a social character,"[5] the station of gentlemen. The sixteenth century saw the schools beginning the task of fitting men for roles that society wanted them to play. A King's College register for the sixteenth century indicates that its men were increasingly changing from the Church to the law and parliament.[6] And once the movement of the aristocracy and gentry to the schools and universities got under way, the schools themselves became associated with the education of the gentlemanly class; they became class preserves. There were various attempts to make them exclusive. William of Wykeham set up a whole series of scholarships for his own descendants at Winchester.[7] In preparation for Elizabeth's first parliament, William Cecil [Burghley] drew up a scheme that would have bound the universities to bring up the children of the aristocracy in one or the other institution. This attempt was not successful, yet the schools and the two universities did in fact become increasingly filled with men of blood. The public schools—formerly open to local boys—were co-opted by the gentry and aristocracy during the Renaissance. Schools like Winchester and Eton taught Latin like the old grammar schools, but they also offered social training similar to the boarding-out system of the Middle Ages. The public schools taught a boy who he was. The boys from Windsor at Eton—often tradesmen's sons—were Collegers: they were educated at the expense of the foundation. The young gentlemen who paid were Oppidans.[8]

During the Renaissance, education became a criterion for defining a gentleman. It became important because it made a man "useful" in a way we have ceased to understand the word. A classical education was quite relevant for a diplomat, a lawyer, or an MP. Raymond Williams speaks of the modern consequences of the educational pattern set in the Renaissance:

> In fact, as the educational history shows, the classical linguistic disciplines were primarily vocational, but these particular vocations had acquired a separate traditional dignity, which was refused to vocations now of equal human relevance.[9]

Latin and Greek were once necessary for the gentleman, and the public schools throughout the eighteenth and most of the nineteenth century deemed that they would always be necessary. The rationale behind the curriculum is very complex and beyond the scope of this essay. On the one hand, it is involved with the whole humanistic conception of the complete man, the *vir perfectus* of Castiglione. It is an attempt to develop the gentleman to the full extent of his intellectual powers. The humanistic scholar Henry Peacham represents this strain in English Renaissance theory: his object as a courtesy writer was to preach the perfection of the individual; the gentleman was to strive to be superior intellectually, and was to be proud of his superiority. Peacham also held to the Aristotelian doctrine of moderation that underlay the doctrine of the amateur: a man of birth was not to go too far in his pursuit of a given subject, was not to become illiberally expert.[10] The educated gentleman was valuable to society as a model of superiority and balance. Roger Ascham, during the sixteenth century, represents a different strain of thought: he wanted to bring the gentleman up to a level of educational competence in order to make him useful to the realm at large.[11] This second strain clearly demands service from the gentleman; a sense of duty was essentially what education sought to inculcate. J. H. Hexter claims that aristocrats in the sixteenth century had come to realize that their claims on public office and administrative privileges were not absolute, and must be lived up to. If the gentleman of blood and rank did not live up to the needs of society, if he were not a competent administrator, perhaps the man of lower birth could take his place. This, in fact, was why the gentleman needed education: to keep his place in society, to prove that he could serve England better than those of inferior birth.

A question arises involving the discrepancy between these two strains in educational theory. Was the educated gentleman "useful" for society because he was a perfected and universal man, or because he was serviceable to the realm? Eighteenth-century theorists divided on the question. Some, like Chesterfield, wanted the best of both tendencies, wanted the gentleman to be a preeminent social model and a competent man of affairs. But Chesterfield sent his son to Westminster to acquire what he conceived to be a gentleman's education and found it sorely lacking; the boy picked up vulgar habits and illiberal traits. The public school in Chesterfield's judgment was not a place to make a man of the world or a man of affairs. Other parents who had less grand designs for their sons agreed that the public schools were unsuitable places for a gentleman. But these people denied the whole notion of public service and the necessity of formal education to prepare a man to assume his role as a useful member of society. In Defoe's *Complete English Gentleman* a mother makes herself clear about her decision not to send her son to a public school:

> No, indeed, he shan't go among the rabble of every tradesmen's boys and be bred up among mechanics. No, no, my son is a gentleman; my son, is he not a baronet by his blood? and he is born a gentleman, and he shall be bred like a gentleman.[12]

"Like a gentleman" evidently means without schooling. The notorious state of the public schools in the eighteenth and early nineteenth century was a perfect complement to parental laxity: the schools, to say the least, were not overzealous in their attempts to form either the complete scholar or the man prepared to assume his civic responsibilities. In John Chandos's masterfully documented study of the public schools, *Boys Together: English Public Schools 1800–1864*, we get an extraordinary picture of places that tolerated barbaric violence, juvenile delinquency, laziness, and the worst kinds of rote learning, cribbing, and pedantry. And genteel parents, on the whole, accepted the schools as necessary proving grounds for gentlemen.[13] Yet there were other people who felt rigorous education had a central role to play in forming the gentleman and man of service. Defoe maintained that the "complete gentleman" had to be a man of education because only a man of education was capable of living up to what was expected of the gentleman: the performance of useful functions. Defoe indicates that younger sons who have careers in law and trade are the backbone of the English nation. The uneducated eldest son is an insult to the word gentleman: he is a man of no use to himself or to others. A man's quality requires an education to support it. And an education makes him more than just another booby squire; it makes him a man capable of handling his affairs, of serving the community, of being a virtuous and honest man. This hymn in praise of education—complete with statistics proving that younger sons are more successful and happy than their elder brothers—takes no account of the true state of education, however.[14] It is a hymn in praise of an ideal.

The reality of education in the eighteenth century unfortunately will not support Defoe's enthusiasm. The public schools had fallen off markedly in their enrollment. Bernard Darwin sums up the situation:

> To give one instance, Eton had three hundred and forty-four boys in 1698. In 1800 it had only thirteen more, although a few years previously there had been four hundred and thirty-six, and by 1825 the numbers had risen to five hundred and sixty-eight.[15]

What was the reason for this falling off (or lack of growth) at the close of the eighteenth century? Answers are difficult to arrive at, but it is possible to cite the unfavorable conditions that might have led to the downturn. First of all, there was a long-standing tradition of violence—of flogging and rioting—that seems to have culminated at this period. During Dr. Foster's headmastership at Eton there was a power struggle between praepostors and masters that erupted into open violence.[16] The praepostors were found out of bounds by the masters in 1768. Claiming the privilege of being outside college because of their monitorial duties, they maintained that their rights were being violated. They held a council of war on the playing field and then proceeded to Dr. Foster with their ultimatum: either their privileges were reinstated, or they would resign their office and refuse to do their Latin declamations. Foster ignored their demands. The boys threw their books in the Thames and marched home. Within a matter of days they were sent back by their parents for an elaborate course of floggings. In Dr. Davies's time, the boys did not accept flogging so readily: they broke up the block and took pieces of it home as trophies.[17] The reign of the famous Dr. Keate (1809–1834) was characterized by more flogging and rioting. No matter what a boy gave as an excuse for a misdemeanor, Keate would say, "I'll flog you for that." Sent word that a group of boys was waiting for him to receive confirmation instruction, he misunderstood the message and flogged the whole class. The boys were not unresponsive: in 1818 they rebelled against Keate, locked him out of his classroom, and pelted him with rotten eggs.[18] The level of violence in the schools also seems to have reached a high-water mark in the early nineteenth century. John Chandos's study reports not only on the brutal flogging system—with older boys punishing their young "fags"—but also on boyish fights that were allowed to develop into manslaughter. With no conception of supervising and monitoring the boys in their leisure time, the schools tolerated, indeed had a tradition of fostering, "liberties" like uncontrolled roughhouse, thieving, food riots, and sadistic games and tricks. Such things were accepted as being part of life—and the school was a microcosm of life's trials, disappointments, violent encounters. Those who endured the rigors and the brutality often praised the system and spoke of the honor and distinction of suffering. One of the most bizarre testimonials was given by Leslie Stephen, Virginia Woolf's father:

> To have been flogged in accordance with traditions laid down from our antiquity . . . by Dr. Keate or Dr. Arnold . . . was to receive an indelible hallmark, stamping the sufferer forever as genuine metal.[19]

Lord Chatham's comment on the public schools is representative of the aristocratic tone of criticism: "A Public School might suit a boy of a turbulent, forward disposition, but would not do where there was any gentleness."[20] The middle classes—particularly those of humanitarian and utilitarian convictions—howled about the medieval barbarism and the antiquated curriculum. Their protests helped form another conception of a school's value and in turn of the gentleman's identity.

Besides the public schools' unresponsiveness to "gentleness" there was the question of their imperviousness to modern life. A curriculum summary from 1766 indicates what a classical education meant—only a classical education.[21] The sixth-form boys had seventeen lessons a week: ten devoted to construing Homer, Lucian, and Vergil, and seven for repetition of passages from the Greek Testament learned by heart. Of mathematics we hear that some of the boys went through "part of Euclid." The authors studied in geography were Pomponius Mela, Cellarius, and Cornelius Nepos: students who could not locate St. Petersburg on a map could nevertheless find minor villages mentioned in classical authors.[22] We hear nothing of modern languages at Eton until the end of the century: a military man was hired in 1797 to teach

French; the boys did not take him seriously, though, because he didn't wear an academic gown. The only part of school life that was taken very seriously was classical verse making. A critic in the *Edinburgh Review* summed up the situation in 1809: "A nobleman, upon whose knowledge and liberality the honor and welfare of his country may depend, is diligently worried for half his life, with the small pedantry of longs and shorts."[23] And being "a scholar" meant only one thing:

> The picture which a young Englishman, addicted to the pursuit of knowledge draws—his *beau ideal* of human nature—his top and consummation of man's powers—is a knowledge of the Greek language. His object is not to reason, to imagine, or to invent; but to conjugate, decline and derive.[24]

A boy's whole intellectual life was sacrificed on the altar of the classics. The results, in terms of educational development of the individual, could be less than satisfactory. Dr. Butler—supposedly a reformer at Shrewsbury from 1798 to 1836—instituted a series of examinations and obtained a reputation as a fine teacher. But Charles Darwin indicates the impact that Shrewsbury had on him:

> Nothing could have been worse for my mind than this school, as it was strictly classical, nothing else being taught, except a little ancient geography and history. The school as a means of education to me was simply a blank. During my whole life I have been singularly incapable of mastering any language. Especial attention was paid to verse making, and this I never could do well. I had many friends and got together a good collection of old verses, which, by patching together, sometimes aided by other boys, I could work into any subject. Much attention was paid to learning by heart the lessons of the previous day; this I could effect with great facility, learning forty or fifty lines of Vergil or Homer while I was in morning chapel; but this exercise was utterly useless. For every verse was forgotten in forty-eight hours. I was not idle and, with the exception of versification, worked conscientiously at my classes, not using cribs. The sole pleasure I ever received from such studies was from some of the odes of Horace, which I admired greatly.[25]

The public schools were still shaping young gentlemen into a pattern that originated in the Renaissance: the fact that what was useful in the sixteenth century was not as useful in the eighteenth and early nineteenth centuries was of little concern to headmasters like Butler. And meanwhile, the classical focus worked to the detriment of other pursuits and concerns. Even religion suffered. At Eton, there was Greek Testament and prayers, but little religious instruction or moral guidance unless we count Dr. Keate's threat to flog boys who were not pure in heart. The boys were left to themselves when not doing lessons. Organized games were rare, and team spirit was certainly not an ideal engendered at Eton at the end of the eighteenth century. Cricket is mentioned along with such games as "Puss-in-the-Corner," "Cut Gallows," and "Hurtle Caps": none of which sounds as if it required any group effort or discipline.[26] It was not until 1796 that the first interschool cricket match took place between Eton and Westminster.[27]

If we are to sum up the "ideals" of the public schools in the eighteenth and first quarter of the nineteenth century, we might recall the remark of the Prince Regent who asked of a man, "Is he a gentleman? Has he any Greek?"[28] The classics connoted social status. A classical education could be a shortcut to gentility; it could give a man a "social character."

The day-to-day reality behind these ideals of learning tended to be a matter of floggings, bullying, survivalist tactics, "liberties" that sound like gross license, individualism, and stretches of unproductive leisure. Such a life was defended with arguments that are essential to understanding the gentleman. Chandos generalizes about the defenders of the young gentleman's liberties at the schools: to interfere with this life of classroom Greek and off-hour roughhouse was to strike at activities that nurtured the "free spirit" of gentlemen. Classical studies and the free expression of one's energies are the essential ingredients in the formed nature of the educated English gentleman before midcentury. Such a conception of the gentleman—at once aristocratic, untamed, unChristian, and barbaric—has been under fire for the last 150 years. The middle class—with its ideas of niceness, order, progress, and Christian respectability—invaded the schools by the 1850s and changed their savage tribalism into something approaching modern regimentation.

As the commercial classes grew and prospered, they needed a form of social validation: education was a more verifiable test of gentility than manners. Mr. Edmund Edmunds, a Victorian tradesman at Rugby, speaking of his boy at school there, made the following observation: "The fact is, if a boy is not educated he cannot keep his position in society."[29] And position in society, in fact, had little to do with knowing how to run a business: an education at Rugby was desired not for its commercial utility, but for the intangible benefits it conferred. Like

Eton, it made a boy unsuited to stand behind a shop counter. An education was now useful in that it gave a boy increased social mobility: it allowed him to claim a place in society and maintain the status of gentleman.

During Dr. Thomas Arnold's time at Rugby, the word gentleman opened out in a variety of ways. An education at Rugby preserved the idea of education for "a social character." Even to the supposedly antiaristocratic Arnold, social prestige was nothing to be neglected. A Winchester man himself, Arnold was concerned with gaining some royal recognition for Rugby, some "mark of encouragement from the Crown" that would offset the school's barrenness of historical associations.[30] He was looking for patronage, the kind of direct attention that George III and Queen Charlotte gave to Eton. He was trying to make the gentlemen of Rugby every bit as gentlemanly in terms of their heritage as Etonians. This is one strain within the concept of "Christian gentleman."

Yet Arnold is justly famous for his attempts to do more than this with the idea of the gentleman. He took issue with the gentlemanly customs in the public schools: with religious formalism, with violence as a way of life at school, with pure classical education, and with the Tory spirit of neglect. Arnold sought to engender "lively moral susceptibility" in his boys, not just a knowledge of Greek Testament. As for flogging, he wanted boys to rise above "its naturally low tone of principle."[31] He enriched the study of the classics with history and modern languages; his teaching attempted to improve on the method of rote learning by emphasizing understanding of a text rather than a mastery of minute grammatical points. And most of all, he was willing to question the past, the whole body of customs that no one cared to stamp out although many were coming to feel that they had no place in a nineteenth-century school. Tom Brown says that Dr. Arnold put a stop to the customs of "taking the linchpins out of farmers' and bagmen's gigs at the fairs, and a cowardly blackguard custom it was."[32] Arnold attempted to suppress the brutal usages of the past like bullying and gratuitous flogging. Thomas Hughes makes much of the expulsion of Flashman—the bully whom Arnold finally succeeded in rooting out of the school.

Dr. Arnold's idea of a school was the idea of a Christian school. Whereas the eighteenth-century public school had its veneer of Christianity—its mumbled prayers, dull readings, sacraments, and unintelligible sermons—Arnold felt a gentleman's education, a liberal education, must be a Christian education: "It is precisely moral knowledge, and moral knowledge only, which properly constitutes education."[33] His preaching—"an image of high principle and feeling," according to Dean Arthur Stanley—gave the boys the consciousness of membership in a Christian society. "It is *not* necessary that this should be a school of three hundred, or one hundred, or of fifty boys; but it is necessary that it should be a school of Christian gentlemen."[34] The Doctor wanted the boys themselves to create this atmosphere. Tom Brown spoke of how he "treats one so openly, and like a gentleman, as if one was working with him."[35] In life as in literature, boys tried to make Rugby what Arnold conceived it to be: Stanley recalls one boy who labored to raise the tone of his particular set for Arnold's sake. And Tom Brown's two great objects at Rugby were to get into the sixth and to please the Doctor.

The idea of the gentleman had taken on a new dimension at Rugby: Christianization of the gentleman was a process that had been institutionalized; the gentleman of Christian principle was no longer just the individual man or the sterling literary model like Sir Charles Grandison. The gentleman that Arnold apotheosized at Rugby could be manufactured: "Gentlemen to Standard," Wingfield-Stratford calls the process; the schools became "character factories." Partly as a result of Arnold's influence the public schools increased in enrollment during the second quarter of the nineteenth century. Arnoldian reformism radiated outward, and Eton finally caught the spirit of the times. Dr. Edward Craven Hawtrey, headmaster at Eton (1834–1852), "a refined and courteous gentleman," came to that college "passionate in his indignation against cruelty" and determined to effect reforms in classical instruction.[36] The reform movement within the public schools culminated in the 1864 Parliamentary Commission Report. The schools were taken to task for their overemphasis on the classics, but were also praised as the nurseries of statesmen, civil servants, and professionals. They were given credit for a function that the eighteenth-century schools could never have claimed: "They have perhaps had the largest share in molding the character of an English gentleman."[37] The schools codified what many consider an improved "social character" and offered it for sale to boys "whose parents are in sufficiently easy circumstances to afford them a gentleman's education."[38] The reference to money cannot be overemphasized; for by Victorian times the public schools had become aristocratic preserves open to plutocratic invasion.

INFLATIONS AND EVASIONS: THE IDEAL GENTLEMAN

7

Another invasion—actually a series of invasions over the centuries, culminating in the nineteenth century in a rhetorical campaign—came from essayists, novelists, and courtesy book writers anxious to offer abstract portraits of the ideal gentleman. As professional and business people found their way into the ranks of the gentry in the eighteenth and nineteenth centuries, the periodicals and novels rushed to provide guidance, uplift, and sermons on the nature of the gentlemanly ideal. Literary culture, religious discourse, and practical literature became congested with definitions, counterdefinitions, prohibitions, appropriations from history, weird analogies, and priggish descriptions. Writers of purple prose unloaded gushing sentiments and baroque metaphors on a public thirsty for a refined doctrine to accompany their money and education.

The "gentleman as jewel" is an image that seemed to appeal to these writers: both James Fitzjames Stephen in 1862 and J. R. Vernon in 1869 were taken with a notion that the true gentleman was a gem. Stephen—a writer who accused Dickens of extravagance and lapses in taste and judgment in *Little Dorrit*—made a case for his belief that the true gentleman was separated from the populace by his moral, intellectual, and aesthetic (i.e., courteous and mannerly) qualities: gentlemen were "picked and polished specimens" of humanity.[1] These specimens, it seemed to Stephen, are indestructible: there will always be gentlemen; there will and must be differences in the aesthetic, moral, and intellectual conditions of men corresponding to their differences in rank.[2] (Here of course Stephen's consideration of true gentility slides back into the old idea that a gentleman was a man of rank. Yet, despite this lapse in logic on his part—he writes abstractly and is dealing with ideals after all—there is something to be learned from his discussion.) The gentleman is a polished specimen and he is "picked." The confused reader may ask—by whom? Presumably by the fate that decrees that one man shall be born a peer and another a peasant; yet this belief turns any democratic talk about ideals in manners and morals into nonsense at best and sham at worst. Meanwhile we are reassured that the gentleman is a permanent social type—not only is he picked and polished, he is—it seems—forever, like a diamond. What more could the reader seek in the way of impressive-sounding, yet empty, generalities?

J. R. Vernon goes a step further, however, and makes his essay into a stuffed-owl item of Victorian prose. One is overwhelmed with jewel imagery. Rank, wealth, power, and show were the mere "setting of the stone"; high breeding, liberal education, easy manners, the absence of shyness, and book knowledge were "the cuttings of the stone"; but the "jewel" itself was a matter of character.[3] Yet the extravagance of the metaphors goes well beyond this. The essay begins by speaking of the gentleman as a perfect whole—"a perfect cube."[4] (At this point it is impossible to resist the temptation to note that this wild metaphor making does not square with the reader's need to be enlightened about gentlemanly ideals: it is all very vague and dissolving; we do not learn much about the meaning or origin of ideals.) In place of an exploration of what such words as "high breeding" mean, we are offered the excesses of Vernon's prose; these reach a high pitch of vulgarity and absurdity when he talks about the gentleman as Christian: "Christianity is the revelation to us here of the Etiquette of Heaven."[5] Such writing can only reinforce a belief that Vernon intended to impress his readers with the grandeur and majesty of it all—which is not of course to suggest that Vernon's remark does not have much in common with what other men had said about the gentleman in the 1830s. Arnold's Christian gentleman is clearly the inspiration behind this rhetoric. And yet Vernon's statement shows us what could result when two ideals were brought together by a writer of purple prose; the grandiose nonsense makes for a blurring of all meaningful distinctions.

Such gilding was nothing new in English prose: when J. H. Newman wanted to present the world's ideal—the gentleman—he turned to a work first published in 1734 and reprinted in 1812; Colonel James Forrester's *The Polite Philosopher* makes similes that match Victorian examples in ridiculousness.[6] It is strange that, in a work that speaks of propriety and claims that "disquiet is the greatest evil," the reader should be confronted after every section of prose with a few stanzas of bad verse that read as if they were intended for decoration. This pamphlet preaches "harmony" and balance and decorum; yet it is at once declamatory in tone and trite in content.[7] The author's intent is to make "vice" and bad manners ridiculous; in the process of fulfilling this purpose, he produces fatuities like the following: "Behaviour is like architecture;

the symmetry of the whole pleases us" or "one arrives at the summit of genteel behaviour by conversing with ladies."[8] (Tracy Tupman, we have found you.) Newman read this pamphlet and evidently found it to be the perfect material for parody. His famous passage on the gentleman performs two key functions that relate to the ideals that we have been considering: it parodies the extravagance of the claims—exposes the shallowness and bombast of idealizers of the gentleman; it also locates the fatal flaw in the ideal gentleman, the absence that made him a performing puppet rather than what Newman considered to be a worthy ideal.

Newman's famous passage in discourse 9 of *The Idea of University* is in one sense a parody of style and substance; it is Newman discrediting the idealizers of the gentleman by caricaturing their subject. He is attempting to demystify the gentleman, to expose him for critical evaluation. He reduces the gentlemanly ideal to absurdity by writing his own purple passage, a stretch of prose that destroys the ideal—for the careful reader—by parodying its pomposity and confusion. Borrowing Newman's phrase, we might observe that it is "almost a definition" of the writers on the ideal gentleman to say that they write in order to dazzle their audience. They promise everything: their ideal is usually a collection of every favorable trait they can think of. They are also emphatic and absolute; words like "never," "best," and "always" are liberally sprinkled through their writing. Their work is literally a spectacle in words: while writers like Vernon and Stephen claim to be examining the internal condition of the gentleman, their prose is all on the surface; everything is showy and grand-sounding; there is much to see—the wild claims, the startling phrases—but little to think about. Newman's parody was devastatingly accurate: he created one of the great put-ons of English literature, an ironic bravura performance staged to show the inflated claims of the gentleman and the inadequacy of gentlemanly traits when they are compared to a higher good.

Newman makes extravagant claims for the gentleman in discourse 9, section 10. The words "all," "never," "too" (i.e., "too much good sense," "too well employed"), and "nowhere" recur and reveal that he is writing without qualification—in the style of Stephen and Vernon. Every trait is magnified, and each quality takes on a certain ridiculous aspect in this pure and inflated form. We have no embodiments of the ideal in this bravura passage, no illustrations—just claims. Like the other courtesy writers, Newman uses striking similes and metaphors: he compares the gentleman to an easy chair or a good fire in social relations and to a sharp knife in controversy. The reader is left with a certain amount of confusion here: how can even an ideal gentleman be so comfortable and yet so incisive?

Taken out of context, section 10 seems to pose a dilemma that has actually been explained in the previous section. In section 9, Newman is speaking about the Christian's humility and the philosopher's (i.e., Forrester's polite philosopher's) pride. In the world of the philosopher, pride—according to Newman—"gets a new name; it is called self-respect; and ceases to be the disagreeable, uncompanionable quality which it is in itself." Newman proceeds to explain how self-respect "subsumes those social interests which it would naturally trouble," how what was once the overbearing self-assertion and pride of an earlier stage of civilization has been softened and integrated into modern community life. Self-respect, in Newman's judgment, has contributed greatly to England's development: "It diffuses a light over town and country; it covers the soil with handsome edifices and smiling gardens; it tills the field, it stocks and embellishes the shop." It is the quality that makes the great world move forever down the ringing grooves of change; Newman makes self-respect into the prime mover of civilization. His devastating comment about this civilized, reasonable virtue comes almost immediately: "It breathes upon the face of the community, and the hollow sepulcher is forthwith *beautiful to look upon*" (italics are mine). Self-respect adorns; it sets the surface of things right. It is concerned with looks, and it belies "the hollow sepulcher," the emptiness within. Why are we confused about the contradictions in Newman's ideal gentleman? The reason is that he is pure surface, and any questions we ask concerning a surface are likely to redound on us; the "ideal gentleman" cannot "answer questions" because there is no inner life to respond to us. The show is everything; if we go deeper, we will find only pride. Newman is discussing the gentleman as an embodiment of the world's values; his concern is to exemplify the poverty of those values. He takes care, however, to demonstrate that the gentleman is attractive despite his emptiness. The gentleman for Newman is a grand illusion, a marvelous spectacle.

While Newman identified and parodied the verbal inflation of courtesy writers, Dickens took on another aspect of genteel language in his attack on people who refuse to speak plainly. Gentlemanly and ladylike evaders—those who will not face the facts of nineteenth-century poverty, crime, sexuality, and power relations—frequently occupy the center of Dickens's novels. In *Little Dorrit,* one of his most incisive and fully developed assaults on mincing speech, Dickens presents a wide range of gentle people who dodge the realities of their society by retreating into blandness, stock response, or prissy phrases. Mrs. General, one of English literature's most famous refined old ladies, is the companion to the Dorrit daughters, the children of a once-degraded but now restored gentleman. She has been hired to enforce the proprieties, especially to shape up the younger daughter, Amy, who has acquired a low taste for work, self-sacrifice, and plain speaking. Mrs. General drills the young girl in genteel speech—papa, potatoes, prunes, and prisms are refined in their sound—and also corrects her severely when she falls into the ungenteel habit of expressing her feelings. A truly genteel person, we are told, maintains a graceful equanimity of surface. Militantly ignorant of the brute facts of existence—especially the agonized history of the Dorrit family—Mrs. General can simply say, "Nothing disagreeable should ever be looked at." A perfectly genteel mind will also not confront the world's beauty; when the Dorrits tour Venice, Mrs. General tells the young girl not to wonder about the city but to follow the "celebrated Mr. Eustace" who "did not think much of it." The ideal lady or gentleman does not experience life intensely: the well-bred person stands at some distance from pleasure, pain, and wonder.

In distilling Mrs. General's character, Dickens sums up the whole frame of mind that chooses to evade beauty and ugliness, joy and suffering: "If her eyes had no expression, it was probably because they had nothing to express." In Lionel Trilling's terms, the gentility of Mrs. General does irreparable harm to her "sentiment of being." When we speak of Mrs. General's sentiment of being, we must stop immediately because we have no evidence from Dickens on which to proceed:

> Mrs. General had no opinions. Her way of forming a mind was to prevent it from forming opinions. She had a little circular set of mental grooves or rails on which she started little trains of other people's opinions, which never overtook one another, and never got anywhere. Even her propriety could not dispute that there was impropriety in the world; but Mrs. General's way of getting rid of it was to put it out of sight, and make believe that there was no such thing. This was another of her ways of forming a mind—to cram all articles of difficulty into cupboards, lock them up, and say they had no existence. It was the easiest way and beyond all comparisons, the properest.

This devastating passage is one of Dickens's major pronouncements on the nature of gentility. The force that keeps Mrs. General going—the central fact of her life, the guiding principle—is her commitment to getting nowhere. The "little circular set of mental grooves" is as disturbing an image as a writer could devise for the conduct of genteel life: for Dickens has left us with the idea that life as conceived by Mrs. General is the negation of forward movement, growth, and progress. To be genteel is to proceed around and around on the same grooves. To add to this analysis, Dickens mentions that the trains going around on the grooves are "other people's opinions." There is nothing left but a set of adopted opinions that make no sense—"which never overtook one another." Dickens changes his imagery toward the end of the passage and speaks in no uncertain terms about evasion: not only does Mrs. General avoid life by getting nowhere in her mental grooves, she literally puts reality out of the way—in a cupboard.

Dickens reveals more about Mrs. General's evasive life as he proceeds with his analysis:

> Mrs. General was not to be told anything shocking. Accidents, miseries, and offenses, were never to be mentioned before her. Passion was to go to sleep in the presence of Mrs. General, and blood was to change to milk and water. The little that was left in the world, when all these deductions were made, it was Mrs. General's province to varnish.

"The little that was left in the world" is a judgment that it is impossible to ignore: for Dickens is talking about a society ravaged by gentility. The proprieties are something more than annoying social excrescences; they are the bearers of destruction; they command the texture and reality of life itself to be gone. The modern reader cannot help but wonder whether Samuel Beckett's novels—dedicated as they are to the "little that was left in the world"—do not reflect an acquaintance with *Little Dorrit:* for if ever a work of nineteenth-century fiction explored the question of a society bereft of meaning and feeling and charged with misery, that novel is surely *Little Dorrit.* Mrs. General is a symbol of the forces that have created this absurd world: the gentility that she represents is implicated in a crime; it has made her life confused and pathetic.

Mrs. General, the repository of genteel values, tells us much about the destructiveness of decorous gentle people. She is a testament to the fact that Dickens did not exaggerate in his representation of a genteel woman. The manner in which the evasions and distortions of gentility have done violence to man's ability to form opinions and ultimately to speak words that carry meaning is not only Dickens's concern. Mrs. General represents a Victorian problem that was explored by numbers of pamphleteers including etiquette and courtesy writers. There is ample evidence that Dickens was dealing with a contemporary social folly in his portrait of Mrs. General. While every courtesy writer is by no means a Mrs. General, while the authors of tracts and pamphlets are not infrequently critical of social usages they observe, the fact remains that they present the twentieth-century reader with a description of—if not an exhortation to follow—certain practices that are Generalesque.

If we begin with the question of the distortion of language itself—and here we are at the center of Mrs. General's activities—we might cite the observations made in *The Habits of Good Society* (1860): the author laments the use of "lady" for "woman" and "hen's companion" for "cock."[9] For our purposes, these usages are pure Mrs. General; but, more significantly, they reflect the author's realization that the whole area of distortion and "evasion" (as the author calls it) is a critical social question that is within the courtesy writer's province. He feels it is his business to analyze what gentle people were doing to the very texture of the language. Certainly such evasive speech was nothing new in 1860. At the beginning of the Victorian period, the issue of distortion begins to receive increased attention in courtesy manuals. In 1838, Arthur Freeling spoke of the misrepresentations of "genteel" people in *The Gentleman's Pocket Book of Etiquette.* Freeling—who was something of a snob—was nevertheless appalled by the genteel uses of language in his day. He even hated the word "genteel" itself; he told his readers that the use of the word reveals that you are not a gentleman.[10] He further notes that the very sound of the word conveys the idea of insignificance. This is quite an admission from a man who advised his readers to strive to associate with "those above" them.[11] Such an admission helps us to place Dickens's contempt for genteel speaking in perspective. It reveals the fact that even intelligent snobs—not to say a great novelist—were talking about the impoverishment and mincing stupidity of genteel speech. Freeling speaks of the horror that many "genteel" people have of calling things by their right names: he tells his reader that he must abandon this horror if "you can hope to be considered a gentleman."[12] In 1838, this writer evidently considered such verbal evasions to be vulgar and lowbred: the pamphlet, after all, was written at a time when Holland House and the old society of free speakers still flourished. The evasions in language became all the more evident as the period progressed.

Dickens's portrait of Mrs. General is in part an expression of desperation: it represents his frustration and outrage about what was happening to language and society. From her distortions of language, we can move to Mrs. General's no less genteel enterprise of stifling conversation. Her comments on the elder Dorrit daughter are to the point: "Fanny at present forms too many opinions. Perfect breeding forms none and is never demonstrative." With such a remark, Mrs. General has dealt a blow to all the feelings and ideas that inform the life of any decent community. It is not possible to talk with feeling or to hazard opinions. "A truly refined mind will seem to be ignorant of the existence of anything that is not perfectly proper, placid, and pleasant." The "truly refined mind," as it were, rejects the idea of a community where people come together to express their emotions and claims on each other. Conversation has broken down and with it the sense that people have anything important to communicate to each other. Here again Dickens was not "exaggerating": for during the Victorian period, courtesy writers frequently warned people to avoid the topic that must always have a primary place in the conversation of people who are authentic; the topic of work was considered low and vulgar. In his attitude toward a "truly refined mind" Dickens reveals his whole attitude toward "good" society: it was for those who wanted to assert status, not those who wanted to be recognized and valued for what they *did*.

Dickens's hatred of do-nothingism is a useful transition to the whole area of gentlemanly activity. Should a gentleman be useful or should he be a seeker of pleasures? Dickens himself—a furious literary worker whose leisure-time pursuits made Lionel Trilling comment that the schedule of his social life was itself exhausting—was strangely poised between social duty and professionalism on the one hand and love of enjoyment on the other. The opposing roles in his life are expressions of two ways of living for the gentleman—service to the community and cultivation of the self. They are our next concerns.

Blood and Property
(Arthur Devis [c. 1711–1787] and possibly James Seymour [c. 1702–
1752], *Leak Okeover, Rev. John Allen and Captain Chester in the Grounds
of Okeover Hall, Staffordshire* c. 1745–7. Yale Center for British Art,
Paul Mellon Collection)

The Estate: The Most Important Expression of Rank
(British School, 18th c., *Pierrepont House, Nottinghamshire,* c. 1708–13.
Yale Center for British Art, Paul Mellon Collection)

Responsibility: Managing the Estate
(George Stubbs, A.R.A. [1724–1806], *Reapers,* 1795. Yale Center for
British Art, Paul Mellon Collection)

Preparation for Genteel Roles
(Attributed to John Zephaniah Bell, *John Gubbins Newton and his Sister.*
Paul Mellon Collection, Upperville, Va.)

Training the Next Generation
(Francis Wheatley, R.A. [1747–1801], *A Sportsman with his Son and Dogs,* 1779. Yale Center for British Art, Paul Mellon Collection)

The Gentleman's World of Leisure
(Arthur Devis [c. 1711–1787], *The Swaine Family of Fencroft, Isle of Ely, Cambridgeshire,* 1749. Yale Center for British Art, Paul Mellon Collection)

Honor: The Pagan Code
(John Sell Cotman [1782–1842], after Robert Dighton [1752–1814], *Caricature of Two Men with Drawn Swords,* 1799. Yale Center for British Art, Paul Mellon Collection)

A Gentling Influence
(British School, 18th c., *A Family Being Served with Tea,* c. 1740–5. Yale Center for British Art, Paul Mellon Collection)

Civilized Companionship
(Gawen Hamilton [c. 1697–1737], *The Brothers Clarke with Other Gentlemen Taking Wine,* c. 1730–5. Yale Center for British Art, Paul Mellon Collection)

Great Fun
(William Hogarth [1697–1764], *A Midnight Modern Conversation,* c. 1732. Yale Center for British Art, Paul Mellon Collection)

The Learned and Well-Bred Man
(Thomas Hickey [1741–1824], *Thomas Graham,* c. 1790. Yale Center for British Art, Paul Mellon Collection)

Sport and the Love of the Countryside
(George Stubbs, A.R.A., *Two Gentlemen Going a Shooting, with a View of Creswell Crags, Taken on the Spot,* 1767. Yale Center for British Art, Given by Paul Mellon in memory of his friend James Cox Brady, Yale College, Class of 1929.)

The Sporting Ideal
(Stephen Slaughter [1697–1765], *Windham Quin of Adare, Co. Limerick,* c. 1745. Yale Center for British Art, Paul Mellon Collection)

Shooting: An Exclusive Sport
(Arthur Devis, *Boldero Brothers of Cornborough, Yorkshire.* Yale University Art Gallery, bequest of Helen Huntington Hull)

Driving: A Non-Productive Pastime
(James Pollard, *John Smith Barry's Private Drag and Grey Team at Marbury Hall,* Cheshire 1824. Paul Mellon Collection, Upperville, Va.)

Companions
(Thomas Rowlandson, *Breakfast before the Hunt.* Paul Mellon Collection, Upperville, Va.)

PART TWO

RESPONSIBILITIES
AND PLEASURES

THERE IS NO UNANIMITY of opinion about how a gentleman should spend his time. Ask a nineteenth-century dandy, a Victorian novelist, a sportsman, an eccentric collector or scholar, a country squire: the conflicting voices and convictions destroy any unitary view of what a gentleman should be doing. And yet, for all the variety of ideal pursuits, there are two recurrent ways of using time that can be extracted from the work of writers and the words of many different kinds of gentlemen.

THE INFINITE NATURE
OF DUTY

8

P. H. Ditchfield, a writer on the squirearchy, helps open a discussion of the nature of duty; he offers the following ideal type: "It was everything to the making and upholding of the country to have in each village and neighborhood a strong man who upheld the principles his sires had taught him, exercised a powerful influence over the minds and manners of his tenants and labourers, was loved and respected by them, and made his house the center of old-fashioned English hospitality."[1] The gentleman had a role to perform in the community that transcended function in the sense of occupation. Although his time was his own, an idle gentleman was widely criticized. What, then, was expected of him? In Ditchfield's words, he was supposed to contribute to the "upholding of the country": he was to exercise "a powerful influence." To clarify this vague expression, we might turn to Benjamin Disraeli; the statesman discusses the term "landed interest," and in so doing provides us with a way of understanding what Ditchfield was driving at in his description of the squire's function. The "landed interest" was not just "squires of high degree," but "the population of our innumerable villages."[2] Disraeli likens the landed interest to a woven fabric: "I mean by the landed interest that great judicial fabric, the great building up of our laws and manners which is, in fact, the ancient polity of our Realm."[3] This building up of "our laws and manners" was not felt by Disraeli to be a historical accident: he was convinced that the stability of England was the result of the responsible efforts of gentleman landlords. The "ancient polity of our Realm" was preserved not by gentlemanly aloofness, but by a clear recognition on the gentleman's part that he belonged to the community at large in more than just a marginal way. The gentleman was more than a manager of estates and a judge at Quarter Sessions; his role extended beyond that of the modern professional, technocrat, or managerial expert.

For a clear, if idealized, enunciation of what the gentleman's responsibility was in English society, we might turn to Washington Irving's *Bracebridge Hall* (1822). Geoffrey Crayon, the narrator of the book, is a guest at an English country house sometime near the beginning of the nineteenth century; he offers his observations on the question of what a gentleman should do for the community. "He can render essential services to his country by assisting in the disinterested administration of the laws; by watching over the opinions and principles of the lower orders around him; by diffusing among them those lights important to their welfare; by mingling frankly among them, gaining their confidence, becoming the immediate auditor of their complaints, informing himself of their wants, making himself a channel through which their grievances may be quietly communicated to the proper sources of mitigation and relief; or by becoming, if need be, the intrepid and incorruptible guardian of their liberties—the enlightened champion of their rights." This notion of the gentleman as benevolent father carries with it the idea of an organic society, one in which relatedness is the key fact of life. Irving was keenly aware of the idea of the gentleman as patriarch; at Bracebridge Hall the resident squire's kinship with his tenants and household dependents is an occasion for the narrator to make a general statement on the importance of preserving the harmonious hierarchies represented by life on a country estate; in speaking of the squire the narrator comments:

> There is no rank of distinction that severs him from his fellow-subjects; and if, by any gradual neglect or assumption on the one side, or discontent and jealousy on the other, the orders of society should really separate, let those who stand on the eminence beware that the chasm is not mining at their feet.

Such a warning is a reminder to the gentleman of the nature of his role and responsibility: he must be sure to remain actively involved with the other members of society; he must not permit the privileges of rank to alienate him from those below.

This ideal of social responsibility was more than just the vision of Washington Irving the American Anglophile. It was embodied in the lives of men of the period. Gentlemen like the famed Coke of Holkham, a late Georgian and Regency squire noted for the great improvements that he effected in land cultivation, made something of a reality out of the benevolent squire. One chronicler of his good deeds sums up his life with the following remarks:

> He lived at a bountiful rate, as gentlemen were expected to do, and he never turned the poor from his door. He served God and fooled no man, as the words carved on his wainscots enjoined. He ventured even into the presence of Royalty in hunting clothes.[4]

Coke was a gentleman of honesty and integrity, and his reputation caused William IV to refer to him as the first commoner of the kingdom. His great popularity was based on his ability to make his own estate into a model of both economic prosperity and harmonious relations. The atmosphere that he created may best be seen in the coming together of local farmers and their families for the great sheep shearing during July 1821. The farmers met on terms of equality with men like the Duke of Sussex. At dinner one of the farmers rose to address the party: "Maister Coke and Gentlemen, what Ah wish to say is—if more landlords would doe as Maister Coke he doe, there'd be less doe as they doe doe."[5] The farmer was saying in so many words that social harmony was directly dependent on the actions of the squires. The loyalty to Coke was a durable emotion, one that was still very much alive in 1841. The supper given to the tenants after the annual audit was held as usual, although his tenants did not expect to see the now-enfeebled old squire. The company rose when he unexpectedly entered the dining room, leaning on the arms of his sons; the men assembled stamped on the floor and sang again and again the "Fine Old English Gentleman." Coke's contribution to the harmony of his own community at Holkham is one instance of how the gentleman acted the role of benevolent father.

The country gentleman's function was to give life coherence and stability. The medium by means of which he acted out his role was the landed estate. For it was his duty to preserve his property as the visible symbol of the social order and to see that life on the land gave each member of the community his place in the social hierarchy. The gentleman had to preserve a continuity with the past; he had to live up to the achievements and contributions of his ancestors. At the same time he had to consider his descendants; he had to leave his properties intact; his reputation for honesty and integrity would also reflect on those who came after him. An estate, according to G. Kitson Clark, was not so much a financial venture as an attempt to make a caste survive from generation to generation.[6]

To make life hierarchical and traditional was the dual function undertaken by men of birth. The nature of country life itself played its part in shaping the gentleman: the landlord presided over a household of dependents and inferiors, a tenantry, and a parish with its poor. The squire was "father" to these: before the inroads of central government—before 1834 with its central board of Poor Law Guardians—the squire was the sovereign member of the community when matters of social welfare were in question. In 1795, a group of Berkshire squires developed the Speenhamland system, and it was to such gentlemen that the poor owed the scanty relief that they in fact received.[7] Welfare in the modern sense of an organized network of public aid to the poor did not exist before the New Poor Law. Along with the Church—which of course was an arm of gentlemanly power—the gentleman and his lady were the first to undertake the task of seeing to the needs of the poor. The individualistic benevolence of the country house was something that the poor had come to depend on. At Hatfield in 1793, five hundred poor were fed twice a week.[8] The fifth Duke of Richmond typifies the gentlemanly role of giver of alms and molder of the social order. He was remarkable for his sense of duty, according to one commentator.[9] His commitment to the weak and poor was a hallmark of his life. He was influential in workhouse management in Sussex; as a guardian after 1834, he personally helped to convince the poor of the necessity for the new law; while trying to resign them to their lot as paupers, he performed the role of entertainer and goodwill ambassador.

> After the manner of a country gentleman, he organized entertainments for them in the park on festive occasions, spoke to them afterwards in his affable, paternal manner, not forgetting to season his bonhomie with humourous remarks about their games.[10]

He was a kind of Roger de Coverley in the world of Chadwick and Ricardo, an old English squire dealing with new English problems of public assistance and state regulation. And his actions—in the context of 1834—are parodic: for "bonhomie" was hardly what was called for in helping the poor in their struggle for decency. Committed as the duke was to the life-style of Old England—to the network of relations between the gentleman and his subordinates—he tried to shape the New Poor Law to his conception of a rural society. He got the parish paupers to accept the nauseating workhouse gruel—"skillygolee" as it was popularly called—by naming one of his racehorses after it. Of the horse and the gruel he remarked, "It was a long time before I could get it to go, but I have brought them both in winners at last."[11] This attempt to compensate the poor for the austerities of the new system—for all its ineptness and inadequacy—was part of the gentleman's role.

Yet, the problems of industrial society as they began to develop in the first quarter of the century were often avoided by the gentleman or dealt with in the simplistic manner of the Duke of Richmond. When we view the gentleman's contribution to aiding the populace during the early Industrial Revolution, we are faced with the fact that "squires" and "gentlemen" frequently did not even see the industrial populace: workingmen were hidden away off the main thoroughfare of Manchester, far from the sight—not to say the influence—of gentlemen.[12]

The willful ingorance and neglect could be traced to vulgarians and patricians alike. In Dickens's *Hard Times* the working classes are in the cold clutches of nongentlemen like Josiah Bounderby and Thomas Gradgrind, the first a work-ethic hypocrite and factory owner who likes to brag about being born in the gutter, the second a hard-bitten pedagogue who hates aesthetic pleasure. The gentleman's studied and willful attempt to ignore the working classes is also recognized by many Victorian writers. Thackeray speaks of his class as having "no community with the poor."

> We never speak a word to the servant who waits on us for twenty years; we condescend to employ a tradesman, keeping him at a proper distance. . . . Of his workmen we know nothing, how pitilessly they are ground down, how they live and die, here close by us at the backs of our houses.[13]

Dickens's work as an anatomist of the gentry was all but devoted to advancing a similar idea: from *Oliver Twist* through his late novels he told stories about gentlemanly failure to perceive the condition of England. In a famous preface to *Oliver Twist* he indicted genteel people for being too delicate in their sensibilities to acknowledge the existence of paupers; by the time he wrote *Bleak House* his anger at "Right Reverends and wrong Reverends" had reached a pitch of brilliance. The death of little Jo, a London street child, is the occasion for an excoriating sermon directed at a do-nothing gentry:

Dead, your Majesty. Dead, my lords and gentlemen. Dead, Right Reverends and wrong Reverends of every order. Dead, men and women, born with heavenly compassion in your hearts. And dying thus around us every day.

When we speak of the rural populace of the period, there is considerable evidence that the gentlemanly classes were gradually set apart from those who used to be their "retainers and even allies."[14] Disraeli devoted *Sybil* to a consideration of the degenerating relations between the genteel and the nongenteel: he felt that the "Two Nations" problem was something new in English history and saw the growth of hostility as part of the gentry's voracious appetite for money and power since the Glorious Revolution; he imagined that the influence of Whiggery and trade had turned the gentry away from its age-old devotion to duty. Unlike Disraeli, we are not looking back to a golden age of "peer and peasant" relationships, but we do submit that the progress of the century saw the erosion of certain ties that existed between the squire and his dependents. The nineteenth century witnessed a marked decline in the fortunes of the landed gentry: regardless of the roseate portraits of the "old English squire" of the 1820s, 1830s, and 1840s, there are circumstances to prove that the gentry was threatened. The nineteenth-century progressive mentality attacked the Corn Laws, and in so doing posed the first great threat to the hegemony of the landed classes. Squires often forgot their "duties" in the scramble to hold on to their property and position. Edward George Bulwer-Lytton describes a "benevolent" squire whose "good deeds" hardly reveal an abiding concern for his dependents:

Sir Harry Hargrave gives away one hundred and two loaves every winter to the poor; it is well to let the labourer have a loaf now and then for nothing: would it not be as well, Sir Harry, to let him have the power always to have bread cheap? Bread cheap! What are you saying? Sir Harry thinks of his rents, and considers you a revolutionist for the question. But Sir Harry Hargrave, you answer, is a humane man, and charitable to the poor. Is this conscientious? My dear sir, to be sure; he considers it his first duty—*to take care of the landed interest.*[15]

This was "the first duty" that Disraeli dealt with so ironically.

Disraeli felt that the Whiggism of modern England with its championing of "Liberty" had severed the connection between the gentleman and the people. The town of Marney in *Sybil* was a laissez-faire society, one where the overlord was a property exploiter rather than a father to his people. The Egremonts had "destroyed the cottages on their estates, in order to become exempt from the maintenance of the population." The aristocrats, according to Disraeli, had abdicated the function of gentlemen. By divesting themselves of responsibility, they had become no more than the ornaments of society. Disraeli's notion of the bonds that should exist between gentlemen and their dependents is often regarded as a vision of an England that never was and never could be. Yet, despite Disraeli's dismal view of nineteenth-century landlords like the Egremonts, despite Bulwer-Lytton's Sir Harry Hargrave, there are actual instances—or rather documents that record instances—of the cohesion, relatedness, and interdependence that was so valued by romantics like Disraeli. Regardless of what they "prove" by themselves, regardless of how "representative" they are, the testimonial verses composed in 1859 by the Percy family dependents help us to understand the concept of duty—and make us believe that it was once a powerful force in men's lives. The great duke's influence on the community is described in the following manner:

> Those relics of the feudal yoke
> Still in the north remain unbroke;
> The social yoke with one accord,
> That binds the peasant to his Lord. . . .
> And Liberty, that idle vaunt,
> Is not the comfort that we want;
> It only serves to turn the head,
> But gives to none their daily bread.
> We want community of feeling,
> And landlords kindly in their dealing.[16]

This declaration of feeling asks several things from the gentleman: it defines what his dependents expected of him. First of all, it asks for bonds between the different orders of society; it also asks for something more than that bourgeois liberty that is merely the freedom to starve; and finally it affirms the values of stability, kindliness, and paternalism. Its plea for "community of feeling" is nothing new in English life, and it leads us directly back to the classic instance of Sir Roger de Coverley, the preeminent literary example of the paternalistic squire.

Sir Roger is "a great lover of mankind." While this is no invariable criterion of gentility, it does allow us to gain access to several ideas that are central to the idea of the gentleman as molder of the community. Sir Roger is a model because his goodness radiates from the social decisions he makes. He is a good man because he is a good master. Upon returning from London he greets his household servants:

> The good old knight, with a mixture of the father and the master of the family, tempered the inquiries after his own affairs with several kinds of questions relating to themselves. This humanity and good nature engages everybody to him, so that when he is pleasant upon any of them, all his family are in good humour.

His dealings with his household are carried through in an atmosphere that is free of harshness or formality. His most conspicuous activities involve the questions that he poses about the welfare of all those in the neighborhood. And his household is harmonious because "his orders are received as favours rather than duties."

This humanity also includes economy. For Sir Roger is the gentleman not only as good man, but also as sensible man. His deeds help to make his little community into an enclave of fair dealing and prosperity. He looks frankly at his own ancestors in the portrait gallery and freely admits the shortcomings of one of them: "he was a man of no justice, but of great good manners. . . . He ruined everybody that had anything to do with him, but never said a rude thing in his life." The fine gentleman's irresponsibility was to be scorned. Sir Roger also rejects the country booby Will Wimble, a man who devotes his life to horses, dogs, and woodland pursuits.

> Will Wimble's is the case of many a younger brother of a great family, who had rather see their children starve like gentlemen, than thrive on a trade or profession that is beneath their quality.

Needless to say, Will's contribution to the community consists of an invention "for improving the quail pipe." The spectator himself laments this waste of the gentleman's ability. "The same temper of mind and application to affairs, might have recommended him to the public esteem, and have raised his fortune in another station of life." Will exemplifies the fact that a good heart was not enough to make a true gentleman. For what was lacking in Will—effort, a sense of duty, a responsiveness to his fellow man—was fatal: it was the do-nothingism that Thomas Carlyle would speak of over a hundred years later. It was a seed of decay in the idea of the gentleman.

The de Coverley papers present an ideal of the gentleman directly opposed to that of the fashionable world. Sir Roger is rejected by a fashionable woman and in turn comes to reject the world of conspicuous expenditure, the sham world of fashion. He speaks of the financial overextension of the gentleman:

> To pay for, personate, and keep in a man's hands a greater estate than he really has, is of all others the most unpardonable vanity, and must in the end reduce the man who is guilty of it to dishonor.

What Sir Roger represents is a style of life directly opposed to that of the gentleman as overconsumer. Sir Roger looks to the past for his ideal, to his ancestor Sir Humphrey de Coverley—a man who was "punctual as a tradesman and generous as a gentleman." This ideal of responsibility and generosity is what Sir Roger takes up in his own life and translates into his dealings with his dependents. He is the man of simple, if eccentric, habits who devotes his life to being the father of his flock, the benign overlord. He enters directly into the affairs of all those around him. In Church he sees if any of his tenants are missing by standing up while everyone else is sitting. His familiarity with those in his parish is so great that he can tell John Matthews to stop clicking his heels in the middle of a Church service. But perhaps his most telling action is the giving of a Bible and a flitch of bacon to the boy who knows his catechism best. For here we have the gentleman as bestower of worldly and spiritual sustenance. This is of course an idealization of the gentlemanly role: the man of blood is seen exerting himself in the maintenance of a hierarchical community; he is shown handing down patronage to an enthusiastic group of dependents. Sir Roger is received with full approbation by the lower orders: he and his tenants are cheered to hounds by the servants

This all-too-perfect vision of gentlemanly duty rang false for many readers; in the nineteenth century Dickens stood the prototype of the good squire on its head by creating William Dorrit, a man of family who is a condescending exploiter of those of lower station rather than a nurturing father. A gentleman of fine tastes and sensibilities who has been confined to the Marshalsea debtors' prison, William Dorrit is Dickens's ironic-pathetic portrait of the way "born" people sometimes live off the efforts of lesser spirits. In the Marshalsea, he lives on the gentleman's—as opposed to the unconnected poor person's—side of the prison.

Dorrit is a pseudopatriarch who makes strained attempts to bring order and harmony to prison life:

> The Father made it a point of his state to be chary of going among his children on the Poor side, except on Sunday mornings, Christmas days, and other occasions of ceremony, in the observance whereof he was very punctual, and at which times he laid his hand upon the heads of the little infants, and blessed those young insolvents with a benignity that was highly edifying.

Dickens also makes a travesty of the squirely ideal in *Great Expectations* as he shows young Pip having patronizing thoughts about the laboring folk in his old village. As a mature man Pip recalls feeling

> a sublime compassion for the poor creatures who were destined to be there [in Church] Sunday after Sunday, all their lives through, and to lie obscurely at last among the low green mounds. I promised myself that I would do something for them one of these days, and formed a plan in outline for bestowing a dinner of roast beef and plum pudding, a pint of ale, and a gallon of condescension, upon everyone in the village.

Most writers were not quite as cynical as Dickens about the gentleman's sense of responsibility. Esme Wingfield-Stratford has explained the gentleman by describing the relation of the squires to their social inferiors:

> They realized that the respect accorded to them was neither disinterested nor unconditional, and that the yokel who touched his cap looked for an answering touchability of a rather different kind in the squire.[17]

This "touchability" is a form of goodwill that came to be celebrated in nineteenth-century literature. There had always been good squires in literature and life; but Wingfield-Stratford has demonstrated that the nineteenth-century squire was idealized, made into a paragon of usefulness and benevolence, brought to a degree of perfection unparalleled even by Sir Roger. The early part of the century was the golden time for the "Old English Squire" in both literature and life; on the one hand, a series of hymns in praise of the squire began to appear in verse and prose; on the other hand, we read of the activities of actual country gentlemen who sound like the squires so extravagantly praised in literature. History and literature run together as the chronicler of reality and the man of letters compete with each other in the description of a social type.

The sense of community and duty are exemplified in the literary portrait of an "Old English Squire" written by Thomas MacLean. Writing in 1821, he describes Squire Careless and the relationship he has built up with his dependents. The squire was well loved:

> For none that called at his paternal home
> Were stinted in forage or sent fasting home;
> As a squire or a hedger were equally treated,
> When each in the parlour or kitchen were seated.[18]

Not only did the squire treat all comers with appropriate hospitality, he also lived out his life in accordance with the principles laid down in the de Coverley papers: he hated London and fashion and he gladly assumed the details of administration of his estate. MacLean goes well beyond the cheerfully didactic spirit of the de Coverley papers by making Squire Careless into an "entertainer-in-chief," a purveyor of good times for all. The squire's wedding is an occasion on which he acts as sponsor of good cheer:

> All the villagers met in the large servants'
> hall,
> And concluded the revels at night with a
> ball.
> For the squire ever liked all around him to
> see
> With broad happy faces and hearts full of
> glee.[19]

Squire Careless was not the only good country gentleman celebrated in bad verse. "The Fine Old English Gentleman" is another verse production dating from the first quarter of the century. Here again we encounter the generosity and public-spiritedness that are the marks of the gentleman as benevolent father:

> And he kept his old mansion at a bountiful
> old rate
> With a good old porter to relieve the poor
> at his gate

Like a fine old English gentleman,
    All of the olden time.

. . . .

When winter old brought frost and cold,
    he opened house to all,
And though three score and ten his years
    he featly led the ball,
Nor was the houseless wanderer e'er
    driven from the hall,
For while he feted all the great,
    he ne'er forgot the small.[20]

The benevolence and sense of duty of this old English gentleman were actually matched by men of the period. In the beginning of the nineteenth century the connotations of the word "squire" were changing: because of the coming to prominence of men like Coke of Holkham, squires gradually ceased to be the barbarians of the popular imagination; to be a squire, according to Wingfield-Stratford, was no longer to be thought of as the hard-riding, coarse booby of the Squire Western variety.[21] Wingfield-Stratford maintains that the behavior of men like the brutal Squire Osbaldestone was atypical of the squirearchy; he argues that the squirearchy was more truly represented by a man like Henry Chaplin of Blankney in Lincolnshire.[22] Wingfield-Stratford cites Chaplin as a "father of his flock" and a "beloved" squire who was the living personification of the Sir Roger de Coverley archetype. Sir Willoughby de Broke said that "no one was half such a country gentleman as Henry Chaplin looked":[23] Chaplin was the portly squire who kept four packs of hounds and hunted six times a week; yet he was also the man who had a legendary reputation for munificence. His hospitality was so great that it was said of him that "when our Harry is broke, which he is sure to be, all the crowned heads of Europe ought to give him 100,000 pounds a year that he may show them how to spend money."[24] He went on at a "bountiful old rate" until he lost Blankney Hall in 1897.

Gentlemanly hospitality was one of the major forces that unified the rural community. Nineteenth-century social histories resound with accounts of splendid entertainments devised by gentlemen for the amusement and gratification not only of their equals but of their tenantry and dependents. The great events in the lives of the gentry—births, comings of age, marriages, deaths—were marked by grand-scale expenditures. On February 27, 1839, the Duke of Richmond's son reached his majority; the event was commemorated by a stag hunt, bonfires, and supper in the great hall for seven hundred of the nobility and gentry.[25] The following day there was a dinner for the tenantry and paupers. The event—including everyone in the social spectrum—was nevertheless careful about rank and precedence without being exclusive: everyone was part of the celebration, but everyone was in his "place." Even the snobbish Charles Greville could see the duke's social strengths:

> Richmond, a very good sort of man and my excellent friend, appears here to advantage, exercising a magnificent hospitality, and living as a sportsman, a farmer, a magistrate, and a good simple, unaffected country gentleman with great personal influence.[26]

The openhandedness of these supersquires was connected with a desire to capture the imagination of the entire community. In 1799 the Duke of Rutland reached his majority. Months had been spent preparing for the three weeks of feasting; tents were set up, and enormous quantities of food were served to everyone from peers to paupers.[27] The menus were carefully graduated to the stations of the guests: the notable guests drinking two pipes of port and forty-six and one-quarter gallons of brandy, the less-notable persons—lesser tenantry, laboring populace—consuming oceans of beer. Such were the distinctions of consumption.

This "old English hospitality" is a recurrent theme in literature: for our purposes, we may view hospitality as "ideal type" behavior; the word refers to "phenomena which recur in a variety of historical contexts."[28] Like the Renaissance ideal of hospitality, the nineteenth-century ideal was also connected with the reputability of the country gentleman's house—and, of course, with pride of rank. In Sir Walter Scott's *Rob Roy,* we encounter a description of Squire Osbaldestone— not to be confused with the real Squire George Osbaldeston—who practiced the "prodigal hospitality of a northern squire of the period, which he deemed essential to his family dignity." Jane Austen describes the same kind of hospitality and generosity in her portrait of Mr. Darcy; she also connects the gentleman's openhandedness with pride of rank:

> Such pride caused Darcy to give his money freely, to display hospitality, to assist his tenants, and to relieve the poor. Family pride, and filial pride, for he is very proud of what his father was, have done this.

A more elaborately described example of this desire for repute is to be found in the prologue to Alfred, Lord Tennyson's "The Princess." The poem opens with the image of Sir Walter Vivian's lawns given over to his neighbors:

> Sir Walter Vivian all a summer's day
> Gave his broad lawns until the set of sun
> Up to the people; thither flocked at noon
> His tenants, wife and child, and thither half
> The neighboring borough with their Institute
> Of which he was the patron.

The gentleman as patron and benefactor offers entertainment on the scale of an amusement park: Sir Walter provides cannons, boats on the lake, a miniature railroad, a telegraph wire flashing messages back and forth. The scene impresses Tennyson; he feels that the gentleman (in this case his own brother-in-law, Edward Lushington) is fulfilling a major function in making his properties the occasional pleasure grounds of the community:

> More joyful than the city roar that hails
> Premier or King! Why should not these great
>   sirs
> Give up their parks some dozen times a year
> To let the people breathe? So thrice they
>   cried, I likewise.

The cheering is a positive mandate not only for the reigning social order, but—ironically and somewhat inconsistently—an acceptance of all that would change the order; the railroad, after all, is a symbol of new fortunes, new men, and "the ringing grooves of change." It is a somewhat jarring note in this idyllic scene of hierarchical bliss.

The gentleman asserted himself and made his contribution to the harmony and stability of the community through such acts of hospitality and beneficence. Yet his leadership in field sports is another important part of his contribution to the life of the nation. The gradual ascendancy of fox hunting throughout the eighteenth century had no small effect on the community at large. While shooting remained the exclusive pursuit of the landowner, hunting had a more democratic tendency. A tenant had to have his landlord's permission to shoot game;

such permission was rarely given to any but the "better" tenants—those who paid the highest rents.[29] On the other hand, by the mid–nineteenth century fox hunting was open to anyone who could ride to hounds. After the amendment of the Game Laws in 1831, the sport was thrown open to the middle classes.[30] Before that time, the sport was in fact the pastime of the squirearchy: the early part of the century was the great era of Melton and the "Quorn"—the best hunting country in England. Those who could afford to go up to Lincolnshire for the hunt, those who could ride with a great master of the hounds like Hugo Meynell, were obviously men of leisure. But meanwhile, the situation was changing. Even by the early nineteenth century, the hunt came to include men like John Jorrocks—a city grocer; amended legislation and good rail transportation made the sport into an activity that included a wide cross section of the rural and urban middle classes. Nimrod summed up the effects of the hunt: "Fox hunting links all classes together."[31] While it may be true that snobbery itself "links all classes together"— while the pursuit of gentility gave Englishmen of very different ranks a common ideal—the fact remains that the hunt was a social and sporting event in which men frequently forgot invidious comparisons in their enthusiasm for the chase. John Conger claimed in 1851 that the chase allowed a chimney sweep to ride by the side of a duke.[32] Class distinctions were less important in the hunt than in other areas of rural life: true enough, various "hunts" were exclusive and reserved for noblemen; yet it is also true that there were many rough-and-ready people who rode to hounds with the gentry. There is even record of a pauper riding with the Pytchley hunt in 1842.[33] E. W. Bovill has noted that the variety of clothes worn at a hunt symbolized the democratic spirit engendered by sport. The master and those who followed him were a motley assortment of people united by a love of and obsession with the chase. A twentieth-century commentator and master of the hounds, Lord Willoughby de Broke, remarked: "If fox hunting had been based on exclusiveness, it would have perished deservedly years ago."[34] As it happened, the sport was balanced between the world of democracy and the world of aristocracy, the world of new men and the world of those whose ancestors had ridden to hounds in the eighteenth century. The sport had a capacity for growth and expansion; it also had its traditional hierarchies. On the one hand, it could absorb new participants; on the other, it required that all submit to the discipline of the master of the hounds—usually a great squire. The hunt was a telling example of how the gentleman of England permitted a once-exclusive pastime to be organized into a pattern that could accommodate and bind together their community.

The gentleman as giver of alms, general administrator of welfare, host, and leader in sport was a powerful force for stability and harmony. He was idealized in literature, and many a historical chronicler has dwelt lovingly on the deeds of actual squires who spent their lives in public service and devotion to the duties of the landholder. Since our major purpose has been to describe the positive contributions of gentlemen, we have necessarily only briefly alluded to the whole literature of criticism of gentlemanly power: Disraeli and Dickens—to cite two critics—were only too eager to point out the undeniable fact that many squires were exploiters and brutal or indifferent landlords.[35] Our object has been to fix on the nature of a gentleman's achievements, his fruitful activities. The system of relations presided over by the gentleman is neatly summed up by Vita Sackville-West in *The Edwardians*. Her character Sebastian, the young proprietor of Chevron, is a benevolent squire devoted to the welfare of those on his estate. He is part of an order of gentlemen

> who, in their unobtrusive way, elected to share out their fortune, not entirely to their own advantage—English squires, who, less favoured than Sebastian, were yet imbued with the same spirit, and traditionally gave their time and a good proportion of their possessions as a matter of course to those dependent upon them. A voluntary system, voluntary in that it depended upon the temperament of the squire; still, a system, which possessed a certain pleasant dignity denied to the systems of a more compulsory sort. But did it, Sebastian reflected, sitting with his pen poised above his cheque book, carry with it a disagreeable odour of charity? He thought not; for he knew that he derived as much satisfaction from the idea that Bassett would no longer endure a leaking roof as Bassett could possibly derive, next winter, from the fact that his roof no longer leaked.

The Christmas scene at Chevron with all the estate children gathered around the tree in the great hall is Sackville-West's way of symbolizing a great squire's attempt to create social harmony.

Sackville-West's images of an organic society distill a literary tradition that has included writers of varying merit and sense. The best idealists—Addison, Austen, Irving, Tennyson—often seem to share the opinions and fantasies of lightweights, poetasters, and rhymesters. While these believers flourished, the idea of creating social cohesion from the efforts of a landed class also aroused scorn, doubt, and ridicule. Thomas Carlyle, the Scotsman bred on the corrosive doctrines of the Enlightenment, was one of the greatest debunkers of the gentry. His anger offers a good way to summarize the best in the antigentleman tradition. A crotchety radical, a plain-living sage who baited sensualists, Carlyle mounted the most potent nineteenth-century attack on the gentleman's uselessness. Living like a puritan and inveighing more brilliantly than any dissenting clergyman, Carlyle—like Swift before him—took on the faults of the gentry while defending the concepts of order and hierarchy. His none-too-consistent assault—mocking aristocratic values while looking for the best men of his time and other ages—makes him a powerfully different writer whose message is no mere localized criticism of contemporary genteel abuses. Inspired by strongmen and heroes, he rejects the gentleman as the sick man of the century.

Carlyle's *Past and Present,* a tract for the times published in 1843, is a fiery affront to gentility. One of the best chapters, "Unworking Aristocracy," uses his characteristic mixture of incisive insult, odd diction, and literary acting out. Impatient with the reasoning of the philosopher or the sustained portraitures of the novelist, Carlyle invents his own fabulous kind of pulpit ranting to discredit the class enemy:

> A High Class without duties to do is like a tree planted on precipices; from the roots of which all the earth has been crumbling. . . . Is there a man who pretends to live luxuriously housed up; screened from all work, from want, danger, hardship, the victory over which we name work;—he himself to sit serene, amid downbolsters and appliances, and have all his work and battling done by other men? And such man calls himself a *noble*-man? His father worked for him, he says; professes, not in sorrow but in pride, that he and his have done no work, time out of mind. It is the law of the land, and is thought to be the law of the Universe, that he, alone of recorded men, shall have no task laid on him, except that of eating his cooked victuals, and not flinging himself out of window.

This passage shows Carlyle flaying the gentleman for his false position in the life of a troubled England.[36] In *Sartor Resartus*—his philosophical-poetic answer to the intellectual crisis of early modern civilization, an attempt to find a way out of materialism and spiritual doubt—he staged another attack on the gentleman, this time on the idea of pleasure as one of the hallmarks of genteel life. His protests against the emptiness of luxury and display provide a transition to the subject of the gentleman's world of consuming and enjoying.

DANDIACAL BODIES 9

In *Sartor Resartus* Carlyle describes the circumstances that cut the gentleman off from the rest of the community. He uses the image of the dandy to work up his critique of English civilization: his chapter on "Dandiacal Bodies" deals with the two nations that have emerged in England. At one point he likens the rich and poor to an electric machine

> with batteries of opposite quality. . . . Drudgism the Negative, Dandyism the Positive: one attracts hourly toward it and appropriates all the Positive Electricity of the nation (namely, the Money thereof); the other is equally busy with the negative (that is to say the Hunger), which is equally potent.

Yet, Carlyle's description of the condition of England contains far more than this mechanical image. "Dandiacal Bodies"—and indeed *Sartor* itself—is a complex network of images brought into the service of social criticism. Carlyle uses the imagery of religion and of fashion to approach the Condition-of-England Question. The dandies are a self-worshipping sect—they live to look at themselves and to read about themselves in fashionable novels, their scriptures. In Carlyle's definition of the dandy, he speaks of a whole group of men who have "consecrated" their every faculty to wearing clothes. These men—almost like saints—"affect great purity and separatism" in their pursuit of dressing; they are set apart from the rest of the community:

> A Dandy is a Clothes-wearing Man, a Man whose trade, office and existence consists in the wearing of Clothes. Every faculty of his soul, spirit, purse, and person is heroically consecrated to this one object, the

wearing of Clothes wisely and well: so that as others dress to live, he lives to dress.

What he requires is attention: the dandy's soul and his social status are both symbolized in cloth. Thorsten Veblen also speaks of dress as "eminently a 'higher' or spiritual need." At the same time dress is an "insignia of leisure."[1] It represents both spiritual fulfillment and social standing. Veblen remarks that "a cheap coat makes a cheap man";[2] he is indicating that clothing is conceived to be a reflection of selfhood. And in a "pecuniary culture," according to Veblen, clothes assert status. Certain kinds of dress prove that a man can consume wastefully, can engage in what Veblen calls "futile expenditure." Here Veblen is not just referring to expenditure of money and cloth, but also of time.

> To discuss for hours the shape of a cravat, to shrink with horror from a badly cut coat, to spend half a day choosing clothes and putting them on, these are moves in a game being played with mock solemnity.[3]

This kind of life—and the ability to sustain it—is what the clothes wearer displays to the world. Veblen writes the following:

> If, in addition to showing that the wearer can afford to consume freely and uneconomically, it also can be shown in the same stroke that he or she is not under the necessity of earning a livelihood, the evidence of worth is enhanced in a considerable degree.[4]

Clothing, then, is one indication of status and life-style. And Carlyle and Veblen both link dress to the spiritual life of the ascendant classes. It now becomes a question of particularizing, showing how dress is related to the gentleman.

A portrayal of the gentleman as consumer should begin with the life of George Brummell. Preeminent among dandies, he is the natural subject for any discussion of dress. Ellen Moers and others have dwelt on his life and maintained that he was a revolutionary in the Regency, a man who was clean and well-groomed in an age of slovenly men and women.[5] The cornerstone of Brummell's creed was "very fine linen, plenty of it, and country washing." He dressed with simplicity, but the essence of his style was that it reflected care and hours of preparation. Noblemen came to visit Brummell in the morning to watch the details of his toilette. This extreme cleanness and carefulness was something new, however. The eighteenth-century fine gentleman is perhaps typified by the youthful Charles James Fox: he dressed in the style of a macaroni, complete with red high-heeled shoes.[6] This was a faddish devotion to clothes for the sake of display and novelty. In Fox's case, it easily gave way to slovenliness; it was not part of a whole "clothes philosophy" like Brummell's. For Fox, clothes belonged to the gentleman as an accessory; they did not seem to be intimately connected with his identity. For Brummell, we are told by Captain Jesse that sartorial collapse and mental collapse coincided.[7] Jesse remarks that, when Brummell was in the care of the Sisters of Charity after his fall, he was not at all responsive to the clergyman on spiritual topics.[8] His spiritual life had ended at the time of his fall from dandiacal preeminence. Jesse says that he may be considered to have expired the day he gave up white neckcloths for black. "I am incompetent to do anything but ruminate over the broken toys of my past days,"[9] Brummell reputedly remarked. To be no longer a dandy was to cease to be a gentleman; to cease to be a gentleman was to cease to be a man.

The emphasis that Brummell placed on dressing represents a particular phase in the social history of England. The Beau was a man who came to prominence in London society in an age that was beginning to think about reform, but had not as yet made the transition from oligarchic to democratic principles. The gentleman's appearance and manners were in the process of being reformed: physical dirtiness among genteel people was increasingly criticized; perfume and jewels were no longer a substitute for hygiene and neatness. The gentleman of the Regency began the task that the Victorians continued—the task of cleaning up and becoming less ornate. Brummell's life was devoted to showing how a gentleman should dress, how he should avoid what was outré, what was in bad taste. His own clothes were simple enough; they emphasized excellence in cut, perfection of fit, and immaculateness. Brummell's manservant frequently appeared with a handful of neckcloths that had been rejected: they were slightly soiled or wrinkled. This fastidiousness was something new in the life of the man of pleasure. In *Humphry Clinker,* Squire Bramble could not stand the smell of his genteel fellow guests in the Assembly Rooms at Bath; for all the showiness of these eighteenth-century ladies and gentlemen, they stank. Brummell addressed himself to the issue: he never used perfume; he never tried to substitute display and splendor for austerity and propriety.[10] Eighteenth-century modishness may be seen in the son of Lady Mary Wortley Montagu:

He diamonds himself even to distinct shoe buckles for a frock; and has more snuff boxes than would suffice a Chinese idol with a hundred noses. . . . But the most curious part of his dress, which he has brought from Paris, is an Iron wig; you literally would not know it from hair.[11]

This kind of bejeweled splendor was alien to Brummell's sensibility. He himself wore no jewels and dressed in a manner that was—for all its excellence—imitable. Brummell made the fortune of his London tailor who proudly displayed the materials that the Beau selected; the Prince Regent himself had no such hold over the fashionable world. While George IV's wardrobe was sold off for fifteen thousand pounds, it never achieved the preeminence of Brummell's simple blue coat. (This perhaps was behind Thackeray's remark that the gentleman was "the man in the jacket.") For all his reputation, Brummell was the man whose dress was not that of an eccentric nobleman, but rather of a private gentleman. It was possible to imitate Brummell because his clothing did not depend on braiding, silks, or jewels. And this, in fact, was part of a revolution that was coming in the dress of gentlemen: the days were not far off when Dickens's Podsnap and a Whig peer would both wear black suits; clothes would no longer set men of birth apart from men of substance; everyone would be respectable and proper in dress who considered himself a gentleman. (Several incisive passages in Richard Sennett's *The Fall of Public Man* distill the new-style gentility of dress in the nineteenth century: "miniaturization"—small details, fineness of fabric, excellence of cut—was the only way that the gentleman was known to other gentlemen on the anonymous city street.)[12]

Brummell helped to set this trend toward uniformity into motion. On the other hand, Thackeray's Barry Lyndon laments the passing of the eighteenth century—an age when the differences between a gentleman and "a common fellow" could be seen; by the Regency, Lyndon claims that there was "no outward difference between my Lord and his groom."

Clothing, then, was not a sure mark of gentility in the nineteenth century, but rather one factor that tended to set gentlemen apart from the other classes. The gentleman was the man in the well-cut suit. While eighteenth-century gentlemen tried to compete with each other for sartorial preeminence, the nineteenth-century gentleman increasingly took to broadcloth in preference to the rich brocades, shot silks, rosettes, and ornaments of his ancestors. The ostentatious dress of Disraeli was considered quite vulgar; Dickens likewise came in for criticism for the elaborateness of his waistcoats. The legacy of Brummell is best expressed by Bulwer-Lytton's Pelham: "Dress so that it may never be said of you, 'What a well-dressed man!'—but 'What a gentleman-lylike man!'" Pelham's sartorial maxims are in the spirit of the Beau: "There is no diplomacy more subtle than dress." Bulwer-Lytton's ironic portrait of the man of pleasure in *Pelham* sums up the Brummellian tradition of carefulness and fastidiousness: "There may be more pathos in the fall of a collar, or the curl of a lock, than the shallow think of."

While Brummell was the man in the blue jacket and brass buttons whom every nobleman of fashion was trying to imitate, there was a part of him that could not be so easily copied. The Beau was an exclusive: he created a little world for himself and shut out all the elements of reality that he considered to be vulgar or stupid. He was set off from other people by his very self-conscious desire to reject the coarse and corrupting influences of an increasingly money-dominated society.[13] He considered the city and its men untouchable. He would not compromise his vision of gentlemanliness and chose instead to sneer at every activity and social usage that fell below the level of his standards. The verbal exuberance that he brought to bear in laughing at his fellowmen is legendary: his aphorisms ultimately alienated him from everyone. The man whose grandfather was a butcher climbed to the top of London society; when he arrived, he found to his great annoyance that almost no one was exclusive enough in dress and manners for him. He had intended a snuff box for the Regent if that monarch had behaved himself properly—if he had been more of a gentleman.[14] Brummell's entire life was spent alienating himself from those whom he considered ungentlemanly. The story is variously told of his having cut his own brother because the latter was not properly dressed. He would accept nothing below his standards, would countenance no coat or wine that did not meet his approval.

Brummell once fingered the Duke of Bedford's lapel and said, "You call that thing a coat?"[15] Captain Jesse cites the instance of Brummell at a nobleman's table calling for champagne: "John give me some more of that cider."[16] Here of course he has the opportunity to "put down" the aristocracy; the exclusive can patronize the man of family and rank. But on a psychological level, we cannot mistake the fact that the butcher's son was compensating for his lack of origins by making a mockery out of the quality of aristocratic hospitality.

There is of course a certain amount of role playing going on in Brummell's life: the reader of Captain Jesse's biography cannot help but be struck by the posing, theatricality, and artificiality of the Beau's behavior in society; he is, as it were, acting the part of the exclusive; at times, we almost have the impression that he is parodying himself. His performing took on a certain silly, absurd quality as it became more and more exclusive. In his desire to put down everything that was below his standards, he literally mounted an attack—and here it is almost impossible to determine what is sincere and what is factitious in his behavior—on the world around him—on things, usages, and people.[17] He claimed to reject modern transportation for parties—he would not arrive in a carriage, preferring to have himself carried in a sedan chair from his own dressing room to the staircase of the house he was visiting. He surrounded himself with the best of everything; his *batterie de toilette* was silver, for, he said, " 'Tis impossible for a gentleman to spit in clay."[18] Captain Gronow, a famous Regency fashionable and grenadier, comments on Brummell's possessions: "His canes, his snuff boxes, his Sevres China, were exquisite; his horses and carriage were conspicuous for their excellence; and, in fact, the superior taste of Brummell was discoverable in everything that belonged to him."[19]

His taste was no less discriminating in people; he cut any connection that was disagreeable or displeasing to his sense of decorum. And he did so with an ease and grace that in themselves set him apart from others. An irate father once reproached him for leading his son astray: "Why sir, I did all I could for him. I once gave him my arm all the way from White's to Brooks'."[20] This is an example of Brummellian decorum: the easy, apparently pleasant and nonplussed behavior that nevertheless is charged with aggression and destructiveness; to be decorous is to know how to put people down—and to know how to get rid of them when they pose an inconvenience. "I did all I could for him": the remark is typical of Brummell; for the Beau to notice and be associated with a man—even for the period of a brief walk—was considered more than such a man deserved; when we say "such a man" it is of little importance who is referred to in the remark; it hardly matters when we are dealing with Brummell's attitudes. He was capable of treating the peer's son and the son of a merchant in the same contemptuous manner. For he, after all, had a power that even noblemen envied; the exclusive could look down on anyone and get a great deal of attention from society for his exclusivism. He had literally created himself, made the butcher's son into the man whose dress and breeding were the talk of London. He made the rules of his own little society—and people like the Duke of Alvanley were willing to follow them. Brummell—as a model of behavior—was a kind of authority figure for Regency fashionables; he had the power to overturn the opinions of noblemen—and the nerve to question and patronize and put down any practice or person that did not meet his dandiacal standards. His career in London may be thought of as one prolonged act of self-assertion at the expense of less gentlemanly men. On being reminded of a five-hundred-pound debt, he made the following remark about his creditor: "I have called the dog Tom, and let myself dine with him." Brummell honored men with his company; a breach of etiquette on the part of a friend—in this case the mention of so vulgar a thing as money—was cause for withdrawal of the honor.

Many people wondered how he could be so absorbed with trifles, how he could take each detail of social life and magnify it. How could he live a life filled with such trivia? He answered Lady Hester Stanhope quite directly on this point; she asked him why he never pursued a higher purpose, and Gronow records the Beau's pronouncement in response to this question:

> Brummell replied that he knew human nature well, and that he had adopted the only course which could place him in a prominent light, and would enable him to separate himself from the society of the ordinary herd of men, whom he held in considerable contempt.[21]

There are several points to consider here. The "prominent light" is the position he attained: a dictator in matters of fashion and dress to London's exclusive society, a companion of a monarch, an equal with men of family and fortune. Brummell "adopted" a course that would raise him to this eminence: he had a peculiar gift not only for living according to what Dickens would later call the "demands of society," but also for increasing those demands and helping to create new ones. It almost goes without saying that he not only trivialized and distorted his own life by his devotion to the demands of good society as he conceived it, but also perished while attempting to meet the demands that he himself helped to create. We see his lonely, pathetic end as a man and a gentleman as a result of his snobbish desire "to separate himself": this classic desire of the snob to be regarded apart from the rest of humanity had paradoxical and miserable consequences—Brummell died friendless, a pitiful object of charity, separate, indeed, at last. The man who had "considerable contempt"—who cut nine-tenths of humanity—had all the brutality and all the pathos of Dickens's William Dorrit.

Brummell acted the part of the gentleman separated from the "ordinary herd of men" so well that he ended his life not having to bother with mortal beings at all. In his last days he used to hold imaginary interviews with the beautiful and long-dead Georgiana, Duchess of Devonshire; she met him on the staircase at his house in Calais and they held court together—two exclusives from a fashionable world that was lost.[22]

Despite a certain personal attractiveness and an ability to use language in an amusingly vicious way, Brummell was a thoroughly small-minded man—one who "meanly admires mean things," according to Thackeray's definition of a snob. Besides the legacy of sartorial excellence, Brummell left behind a reputation for haughtiness that connected him with Thackeray's world of snobs. Brummell leads us from the world of the gentleman as mannequin to the world of the gentleman as snob. Snobbery was the full-time activity of many gentlemen: they spent their time, like Brummell, preserving minor and major social distinctions and endeavoring to set themselves apart from ungenteel people by their fashionable practices. To the snob, gentility did not carry duties and require a man to be related to his equals and inferiors; it was a condition that was maintained by open hostility to all but certain "recognized" persons. "I can bear it no longer—this diabolical invention of gentility which kills natural kindliness and honest friendship." Thackeray felt that gentlemen snobs were a threat to the progress of human community in England, were making British society into separate groups dedicated to exclusivism; meanwhile, more and more people were trying to ape the manners of the hereditary aristocracy. He described English society in two words: "Toadyism, organized." "O free and happy Britons, what a miserable, truckling, cringing race you are!" he wrote in "A Shabby Genteel Story." He devoted *The Book of Snobs* to developing this notion. To begin with, he felt that "fashionable," "exclusive," and "aristocratic" should be banned from honest vocabularies. The *Peerage* is the Englishman's second Bible, and Thackeray laments the "lordolatry" of men who eagerly devour the Court Circular. He finds that the lack of connectedness between the classes in English society is the result of the exclusiveness of the nobility; for an example, he cites the fact that the community has been divided in spiritual matters:

I read in the newspapers that the Right Reverend the Lord Charles James administered the rite of confirmation to *a party of the juvenile nobility* at the Chapel Royal—as if the Chapel Royal was a sort of ecclesiastical Almack's and the young people were to get ready for the next world in little exclusive genteel knots of the aristocracy, who were not to be disturbed in their journey thither by the company of the vulgar.

The "company of the vulgar" was the snob's greatest fear: he did everything to separate himself from those below him. The snob, after all, was engaged in the enterprise of "moving in society"; any connection that would tend to bring him down in the hierarchy was to be shunned. Thackeray describes Lady De Mogyns (formerly Muggins) whose progress in society "may be traced by the sets of friends she has courted, and made, and cut, and left behind." To "cut" and "leave behind" were the snob's characteristic activities; in the case of Sir Alured Mogyns Smith, second Baronet—Thackeray always loved "a good name" and had a marvelous ability to think up these pretentious concoctions—we have a characteristic example of leaving one's family "behind"—getting rid of "Muggins" and assuming a Norman name. Thackeray elaborates this process of "cutting" an ungenteel past by describing how money literally used to be laundered:

> It used to be the custom of some very old fashioned clerks in the City, when a gentleman asked for change for a guinea, always to bring it to him in washed silver: that which had immediately passed from the hands of the vulgar being considered as too coarse to soil a gentleman's fingers. So, when the City snob's money has been washed during a generation or so; has been washed into estates, and woods, and castles, and town mansions, it is allowed to pass current as real aristocratic coin. Old Pump sweeps a shop, runs on messages, becomes a confidential clerk and partner. Pump the Second becomes a chief of the house, spends more and more money, marries his son to an Earl's daughter. Pump Tertius goes on with the bank; but his chief business in life is to become the father of Pump Quartus, who comes out a full-blown aristocrat, and takes his seat as Baron Pumpington, and his race rules hereditarily over this nation of snobs.

Thackeray sees the making of a genteel family as a snobbish activity. For the creation of Baron Pumpington means "that there should be a race *set apart* [italics mine] in this happy country, who shall hold the first rank, have the first prizes and chances in all government jobs and patronage." The idea of apartness is central to climbing in society—a man attempts to separate himself and occupy a height along with a select few. Snobs thus had to spend their time seeing that their position in society was not being infringed upon, that they were indeed quite separate from the vulgar people one notch lower in the hierarchy.[23] Thackeray sees society as a series of interlocking acts of condescension: each person protecting his gentility by patronizing those below.

> Will the Duchess of Fitzbattleaxe (I like a good name) ever believe that Lady Croesus, her next door neighbor in Belgrave Square, is as good a lady as her grace? Will Lady Croesus ever leave off pining for the Duchess' parties, and cease patronizing Mrs. Broadcloth, whose husband has not got his Baronetcy yet? Will Mrs. Broadcloth ever heartily shake hands with Mrs. Seedy, and give up those odious calculations about poor dear Mrs. Seedy's income? Will Mrs. Seedy, who is starving in her great house, go and live comfortably in a little one, or in lodgings? Will her landlady, Miss Letsam, ever stop wondering at the familiarity of trades-people, or rebuking the insolence of Suky, the maid, who wears flowers under her bonnet, like a lady?

A key way that the snob had of separating himself from vulgar people was the ritual of dinner giving. Thackeray is again one of the most vivid chroniclers of this gentlemanly activity. In "A Little Dinner at Timmins's" a sumptuous array of food and drink is provided by a middle-class gentleman to impress his superiors; Thackeray's point is that the gentleman in question has gone to tremendous expense and trouble to entertain a group of strangers who have no claim on him except that his wife considers them to be genteel. Friends and relatives are slighted in the process of putting up a front for the world. Thackeray further deals with such "dinner-giving snobs" in *The Book of Snobs;* he criticizes a "man who goes out of his natural sphere of society to ask lords, Generals, Aldermen, and other people of fashion, but is niggardly of his hospitality towards his own equals. . . ." This kind of entertaining is not hospitality, but display. It is done in the spirit of exclusivism: people are summoned by invitation to partake of expensive food and drink with the express purpose of showing the community who is included and who is excluded. To be asked to a fashionable gentleman's table is to be accepted by society. Brummell's remark that he "let himself dine with" a certain man is clear indication that dinner invitations confer the notion of equality and that such invitations are to be prized for their snob value. The monetary value of the food set before the guests was of the greatest importance—it was a measure of the host's gentlemanliness. Thorsten Veblen wrote of the gentleman that he "becomes a connoisseur in creditable viands of various degrees of merit, in manly beverages and trinkets, in seemly apparel and architecture, in weapons, games, dances, and the narcotics."[24] The culinary phase of conspicuous consumption has been variously discussed: Phillipa Pullar's *Consuming Passions* illustrates how the English gentleman's taste in food and drink was a correlative of social status and how eating habits distinguished the gentlefolk from the commonality.[25] J. B. Priestley, in *The Prince of Pleasure,* also deals with the question of food; he reproduces a dinner menu for 1817 at the Royal Pavilion, Brighton: the bill of fare indicates that The First Gentleman of Europe favored French dishes; the multitude of courses and the complicated preparation required for such items as *le jambon à la broche, au Madère* are indicative of the fact that food was also a hallmark of gentility.[26] The Regency is a period of great chefs—men like Francatelli and Ude established their reputations by preparing the elaborate fare that gentlemen regarded as part of the life of a man of quality. A club like Watier's—Brummell's club—was made famous by its chef and its policy of giving suppers to the men at the gaming tables.

Food and drink, however, were not the only ways the man of pleasure had of consuming genteelly. Fundamentally, dress, snobbery, and dining were ways of filling time in a gentlemanly manner. Veblen's chapter on "Conspicuous Leisure" is helpful in understanding the mentality of men who lived unproductive existences. He begins by explaining that leisure is not indolence or quiescence, but nonproductive consumption of time.[27] The gentleman used time in this way for two reasons: first, because of a sense of the vulgarity of productive work; second, because unproductive use of time was evidence of the ability to afford a life of idleness. Since leisure, as distinguished from exploitation, does not commonly result in a material product, it is necessary for the gentleman to account for his time and to show that he has used leisure reputably (i.e., genteelly), Veblen's theoretical explanation provides a frame of reference for different actual accounts that we discover of gentlemanly waste of time and conspicuous consumption. P. H. Ditchfield, an early twentieth-century writer on the squirearchy, quotes an eighteenth-century squire on the subject of the fashionable gentleman's day:

Those useful hours that our fathers employed on horseback in the fields are lost to their posterity between a stinking pair of sheets. Balls and operas, assemblies and masquerades, so exhaust the spirits of the puny creatures over night, that yawning and chocolate are the main labours and entertainments of the morning. The important affairs of the barber, milliner, perfumer, and looking glass are their employ till the call to dinner, and the bottle or the gaming table demands the tedious hours that intervene before the return of the evening assignations.[28]

Ralph Nevill, in his book *The Man of Pleasure,* gives a picture of the daily life of a Regency man of pleasure: the gentleman begins the day lolling in bed, reading papers, going to Truefett's and having his hair brushed, waiting to dine out. When the possibility of a profession is mentioned, a certain young man makes the following reply:

He thought he would rather drive a hansom, because there seemed less boredom about it than about anything else: one would not have to get down and if one wanted to talk, one had only to open the hole in the roof of the cab.[29]

During the Regency it was considered quite genteel to drive coaches: a craze for fast driving, the pleasures of the open road, and the freedom from responsibility that such an existence carried made it appealing to many noblemen bored with the round of dinners and balls that were the usual lot of the privileged. Lord Ailesbury's great ambition was to be taken for a cab driver. We will return to the subject of gentlemen and their fascination with lowlife, but for the moment we must continue the subject of uses of time.

A fashionable "sprig" turned to a multitude of pleasures to fill his hours. Mr. Nevill has uncovered a parody of a blue book—an imaginary interview not with a factory worker or pauper, but with a young peer:

The scion of a noble race said that he had been in the House of Peers twice; though once was for a bet. Had been educated. Had gone to Eton, where he had got well kicked with no bad results, and then to Oxford. When there, was at Christ Church. Did not take a degree, but instead wore a velvet cap with a gold tassel, and kept horses. Wore also a ribbed silk gown. On high days wore a rich figured silk covered with large gold patches, and dined at a high table with "Dons." Spent 5,000 pounds at Oxford, and left when he was twenty one. Yes, he had lots of ancestors. Considered it "great fun" to be a hereditary legislator. Did not care what was disestablished as long as it was not "Tattersalls." No, did not know there had been a row in the Commons about the Irish Church. Should vote against the Suspensory Bill, because someone he knew wanted a berth over there in the clerical line. Has no prejudices on the question. Would give the Commissioners long odds on the result. Considered the House of Lords a "grand institution." Saw something about "thanking God there was a House of Lords" in last week's *Bell's Life,* and thought it great fun. Should send his vote up by proxy. Did not care much what happened, as long as it did not interfere with grouse shooting, the Derby Day, or Rotten Row. Knew some good fellows in the Commons, though he thought they talked too much. Had heard of Oliver Cromwell. He ran fifth for the Chester Cup in '61.[30]

The object of his existence was to have "great fun," to help his friends to places, and to trouble himself as little as possible.

Such a young gentleman with his time wasting and expenditures brings us to the world of Thackeray's *Yellowplush Papers.* Mr. Deuceace, the son of the Earl of Crabs, is a barrister, but he does not regard his profession as his major activity: "the young gnlmn was a gnlmn," his servant Charles reminds the reader. "He kep a kab—he went to Holmax—and Crockfuds—he moved n the most xquizzit suckles— and trubbled the law boox very little, I can tell you." Deuceace, like the blue book peer, has run up debts, and Charles comments that "to know even what a real gnlmn *owes* is somethink instructif and agreeable." The more fashionable you are, the more money you owe, and Deuceace has spent his days since youth becoming fashionable. His debts include Crockford's 3,711 pounds, 4,963 pounds in IOUs, 1,306 pounds in tailors' bills, and bills "contracted at Cambritch" amounting to 2,193 pounds. To make up for some of these losses, Deuceace takes to a life of gambling.

The card table was another way of consuming time genteelly. Much of Thackeray's early work deals with the gentleman as gambler. Honor in the sense of honesty means nothing to such men: Thackeray describes the selfishness and unscrupulousness of Deuceace's world. Yellowplush comments on his master: "If he had been a common man, you'd have said he was no better than a swindler. It's only rank and buth that can warrant such singularities as my master show'd." In seeking pleasure and self-aggrandizement, the "gnlmn" Deuceace victimizes his friends: he is the snob and cheat as gentleman. Yellowplush, however, knows that this world of fashionable men is a world apart:

"But, in coarse, it's not for us to judge our betters;—these people are a superior race, and we can't comprehend their ways." Thackeray's Barry Lyndon is also part of this superior race, and gaming constitutes his major activity. He feels that the man of the baize is a superior being, that gambling is a genteel occupation:

> I knew I was born a gentleman, from the kindly way in which I took to the business; as business it certainly was. For though it *seems* all pleasure, yet I assure any low-bred person who may chance to read this, that we, their betters, have to work as well as they: though I did not rise until noon, yet had I not been up at play until well past midnight?

Barry "knew" he was a gentleman because he took to playing with such ease and relish: the curious aspect about play—what is somewhat paradoxical—is that it is considered by this gentleman to be both work and play at the same time; yet it is a "business" that separates Barry from "low-bred persons" because it is not pursued during "business hours"; on a more complex level, it is a "business" that does not seem to require industry, strenuous effort, or neglect of pleasure. And, of course, Veblen's concept of nonproductive use of time is not quite adequate to describe the nature of this gentlemanly "business," for Barry is making profits while playing. He is Huizinga's *homo ludens:* Barry the gambler is free of the responsibilities, the duties, and the rationality of any business or profession; he is a man playing for the adventure of play and for the genteel income that he gains from his efforts. Barry would not spend his time in a profession like the army with a lot of "low fellows." Neither would he use his hands to earn his living, even in a time of desperation: "I could not soil my fingers by manual occupation." He is instead the gallant gentleman who sits down before the baize and challenges all comers. Lyndon justifies his life-style by reminding the reader that the prejudices of nineteenth-century men against play are vulgar and unworthy of gentlemen; he laments the decline of the genteel world of the eighteenth century—a world where deep play was accepted as a matter of course.

> In later times a vulgar national prejudice has chosen to cast a slur upon the character of men of honour engaged in the profession of play; but I speak of the good old days of Europe, before the cowardice of the French aristocracy (in the shameful Revolution, which served them right) brought discredit and ruin upon our order. They say fie upon men engaged in

play; but I would like to know how much more honourable *their* modes of livelihood are than ours. . . . It is a conspiracy of the middle classes against gentlemen: it is only the shopkeeper cant which is to go down nowadays. I say play was an institution of chivalry: it has been wrecked, along with other privileges of men of birth.[31]

Barry looks back to the world where Charles James Fox gambled away 140,000 pounds before he was twenty-five, the world where Georgiana, Duchess of Devonshire, played so deeply that even her husband could not find out the extent of her debts. In *The Four Georges,* Thackeray capsules that world in one quotation from Seymour's "Court Gamester":

> Gaming has become so much the fashion that he who in company should be ignorant of the games in vogue would be reckoned low-bred, and hardly fit for conversation.

In *The Book of Snobs* he sums up the magnitude of the gambling phenomenon by telling the reader that many fine gentlemen spent one-third of their lives playing whist in the clubs.

Clubs and assembly rooms were another aspect of fashionable life that made the society of gentlemen exclusive. E. Beresford Chancellor's *Memorials of St. James's Street* gives the history of gentlemen's clubs like White's, Brooks', Boodle's, and Crockford's. Gaming was the principal activity at these clubs in the eighteenth and early nineteenth centuries. White's was founded in the late seventeenth century as a chocolate house, but gradually achieved an exclusive reputation and strictly limited its membership.[32] The club set down its rules in 1743: members were admitted by ballot, one black ball was enough for exclusion, and each member had to contribute a guinea a year toward keeping a good cook. The club was run in the late eighteenth century and early nineteenth century by George Raggett, an industrious businessman who found that his exclusive patrons frequently dropped fortunes at the gaming tables. Raggett also found it worth his while to wait up until play was over: he would sweep the floor and pick up the stray monies that fell from the tables. White's was the club of fashionable gentlemen from Horace Walpole to Lord Palmerston. It was exclusive and suited to the tastes of men who desired to spend large amounts of time on gaming. Chancellor quotes Bramston's *Man of Taste* (1733) to good effect:

> Had I whole countries, I to White's would go,
> And set land, woods, and rivers at a throw.[33]

Many gentlemen felt this way. They spent evenings betting on the possibilities of a man's living or dying, of the possibility of a fashionable marriage taking place. The atmosphere of the club drew together men who were the same rank and wanted to consume time together. At Brooks's the situation was the same: once Charles James Fox and Fitzpatrick played cards from ten at night to six in the morning. The club remained the social headquarters of the Whigs and Liberals well into the nineteenth century: it witnessed Fox's spectacular gambling defeats and was famed for the hospitality that it offered to Edmund Burke, Walpole, Edward Gibbon, and Sir Joshua Reynolds. The reputation of Crockford's also rested on the deep play that went on: Captain Gronow even claimed that all the ready money for the Regency generation passed into the coffers of the club.[34] Gaming and dining on the specialties of the famous chef Ude were the attractions.

Of all the gathering places of fashionable gentlemen in the early nineteenth century, it was Almack's Assembly Rooms that achieved the highest reputation for exclusiveness. Captain Gronow wrote the following about the great period of Almack's popularity, the era just after the Napoleonic wars: "One can hardly conceive of the importance which was attached to getting admission to Almack's, the seventh heaven of the fashionable world."[35] The Assembly Rooms did not offer luxurious refreshments, splendid surroundings, or the excitement of gaming. What they did offer was a company of people who were considered to be the most fashionable men and women in London. The club had several patronesses including Sarah, Lady Jersey, the Princess Leven, and the Princess Esterhazy: these ladies decided on admission and set the rules to be observed. Gronow says that

> very often persons whose rank and fortunes entitled them to the entree anywhere were excluded by the cliquism of the lady patronesses, for the female government of Almack's was a pure despotism and subject to all the caprices of despotic rule. It is needless to add that, like every other despotism, it was not innocent of abuses.

Almack's could turn away the Duke of Wellington because he arrived after hours or improperly dressed: the patronesses maintained the right to exclude anyone, regardless of rank or wealth, who did not meet their standards of *ton*. *Ton* is a vague word that got bandied around rather frequently during the Regency, but to be *haut ton* was prerequisite for admission to Almack's: a gentleman had to have fashionable credentials. To be acceptable a man could be an exquisite like Brummell, a gentleman of rank and achievement like Wellington, or a clever aphorist and light-verse writer like Henry Luttrell: he always, however, had to be a fashionable—a gentleman set apart from the rest of the community by his manners and associations. Membership in Almack's was one criterion by which a gentleman's fashion and quality were judged: Henry Luttrell sums up the importance of acceptance in his famous lines from "Advice to Julia":

> If once to Almack's you belong
> Like monarchs you can do no wrong;
> But banished thence on Wednesday night,
> By Jove, you can do nothing right.[36]

The Assembly Rooms even became the occasion for an 1827 novel called *Almack's*.[37] Mr. Chancellor quotes liberally from the novel, which is an attack on an institution that the author considered to be foolish and harmful in its exclusivism: "Almack's is a system of tyranny which would never be submitted to in any country but one of such freedom that people are at liberty to make fools of themselves." The major activity of the Rooms seems to have been the snobbish business of keeping people out. The novel *Almack's* contains an "Advertisement" for patronesses that sums up the spirit of hostility and haughtiness that characterized the institution.

> The patroness must possess great tact, in order to be able to practice with precision the different degrees of *the art of cutting,* which last qualification must be a *sine qua non* previous to any attempt to enter as candidate.[38]

Dickens's attitude toward the meanness and absurdity of genteel gatherings is expressed in Mr. Pickwick's visit to Bath. The master of ceremonies at the Assembly Rooms—Angelo Cyrus Bantam, Esquire—describes the social life of the watering place:

> The ball nights at Ba-ath are moments snatched from Paradise, rendered bewitched by music, beauty, elegance, fashion, etiquette, and—and—above all, by the absence of tradespeople, who are quite inconsistent with

Paradise; and who have an amalgamation of themselves at the Guildhall every fortnight, which is, to say the least, remarkable.

Pickwick does not think much of this exclusive society. He refers to the Dowager Lady Snuphanuph as a "fat old lady." Meanwhile Lord Mutanhed tries to stare Pickwick down. This first of Dickens's do- and know-nothing aristocrats is a fashionable who drives mail carts and says "Veway" for "very" in accordance with true aristocratic speech. He is the richest man at Bath, and thus sought after by Mrs. Colonel Wugsby's second daughter; her first daughter has been forbidden to dance with a man whose father's eight hundred pounds dies with him.

Dickens, like Thackeray, brings broad humor and humanity to bear on this snob society. His agent for showing up the society at Bath for all its fatuousness and ceremonious rigidity is Sam Weller. The gentleman's servant is left to show gentlemen that the code by which they are living is absurd. Sam's decency and common sense—not to mention his use of irony—serve to expose the pretense of watering-place society. Thackeray was probably so taken by the character of Sam that he created Charles Yellowplush—another servant who offers criticism of the genteel world. *The Yellowplush Papers* was published from 1837–39. Thackeray had had time to assimilate Sam's message—that exclusivism was ridiculous and was parodied by servants themselves. Dickens's scenes at Bath involve Sam with a very genteel set of domestics; here he makes a mockery of their values. Like Yellowplush after him, he shows that the pettiness and snobbery of the servants is a miniaturization of the snobbery of gentlefolks. Sam receives an invitation to Mr. Smauker's soiree; he is presented with all the trappings of gentility—a "select" company, a good dinner, and late hours. The "swarry" and its exclusiveness are deflated by Sam who comments that he never heard of "biled mutton called a swarry before."

Everything that the gentleman of fashion did with his time, however, was not *haut ton*. Our modern term "slumming" accurately describes several important pursuits that the man of pleasure and fashion engaged in when he was not dressing, being a snob, dining, gaming, or visiting the clubs of St. James's Street. Our purpose here is certainly not to exhaust all the "low pursuits" that gentlemen sought out in London. Such an undertaking would involve everything from bear baiting to prostitution.[39] It seems more appropriate—and it will prove more directly illustrative—to focus on one text that deals with the young gentleman discovering the variety of pleasures of the metropolis: Pierce

Egan's *Real Life in London*. This loosely put together narrative describes the adventures of Tom Dashall and Bob Tallyho, the former a London fashionable at the beginning of the book, the latter a country gentleman come to town to learn about "Life." Tom takes Bob under his tuition, and together they set out to encounter London's pleasures. They meet up with Charles Sparkle, Esquire—a fashionable man with great knowledge of the world. But the primary purpose of the narrative is to take the two young men through a tour of the pleasure haunts of the city. Egan wants to show what young gentlemen considered "great fun." He defines the expression BON TON, and in so doing describes the ethos of the man of pleasure adrift in the city:

> Bon Ton's to swear, break windows, beat the
> Watch
> Pick up a wench, drink health, and roar a
> catch.[40]

This conception of the gentleman's occupation causes Egan to give such young men the name "dashers." The section called "How to Cut a Dash" tells the young gentleman never to "think of following any business or profession,—such conduct is unworthy of a dasher." The dasher is basically an idle ruffian, in Egan's view; he is fashionable, but not a true gentleman because he has no manners or breeding.

> To resemble his groom and his coachman is his highest ambition. He is a perfect horseman, a perfect whip, but takes care never to be a *perfect gentleman*. His principal accomplishments are sporting, swaggering, milking, drawing, and greeking.[41]

The dasher loves unscrupulous horseplaying ("milking") and cheating at cards ("greeking"). He is often a man of birth and has often had the education of a gentleman. Tom and Bob meet a Westminster boy who is a perfect example of the gentleman dasher; in Tothill Fields the boy learned "slang" and "lewdness":

> He has likewise a fine opportunity of contracting an unalterable penchant for the frail sisterhood, *blue ruin,* milking, cock fighting, bull and badger baiting, donkey racing, drinking, swearing, swaggering, and other refined amusements, so necessary to form the character of an accomplished gentleman.[42]

Westminster was obviously a place to learn the pursuits of a dasher: it was, we might recall, the school from which Lord Chesterfield removed his son.

Egan goes on to describe other activities and accomplishments "absolutely necessary to the finished gentleman of the present day." He uses Mr. Spankalong as an example of a mail-coach gentleman who fits the pattern of the dasher; Spankalong is dressed in "a green coat, cut in the true jockey style, so as to render it difficult to ascertain whether he is a gentleman or a gentleman's groom."

> This gentleman has a most unconquerable attachment to grooms, coachmen, and stable assistants; whose language and manners is one of the principal studies of his life to imitate. . . . He will take a journey of a hundred miles out of town, merely to meet and drive up a mail coach, paying for his own passage, and feeling the coachman for permission. . . . And it is a fact, that he had one of his teeth punched out, in order to enable the noble aspirant to give the true coachman's whistle.[43]

This fashionable man of pleasure—fashionable because of his rank, his freedom from work, and his dashing and adventurous style—was, of course, not an exclusive: he took his pleasures with men of low birth and cared nothing for polished manners. Yet he was by no means an integral part of the community: he had no duties to perform; he spent his time seeking out thrills that would stimulate an imagination jaded by too much privilege and money. It was only natural that when the gentleman was surfeited with the world of exclusive clubs and assemblies he would turn to the opposite end of the social spectrum for new experiences. That the exclusive on St. James's Street could turn into the dasher who frequented the hells of the East End was not surprising. Even Bulwer-Lytton's fastidious, dandiacal Pelham did not mind spending a riotous night drinking blue ruin (gin) and consorting with low company.

Pierce Egan's Tom Dashall and Bob Tallyho watch the pleasures of dashers, but they never become directly involved in fashionable lowlife. Their purpose has been to observe "men and manners" and to see "Life." Tom, who has "mingled in all ranks and degrees of society, was able to associate himself with the high or the low, as circumstances require, and to form tolerably accurate estimates of those by whom he was surrounded."[44] Dashall was once a fashionable, Egan tells us, but through experiencing scenes of riot and debauchery he has become "a steady, contemplative young man; a peripatetic philosopher; bored with the scenes of *ton,* and deriving pleasure only from the investigation of Real Life in London." He has not become, despite his name, a dasher: he is a gentleman observer, watching the pleasures of the metropolis, yet content to remain an outsider. He is only looking for "substantial information and rational amusement": he has no desire to participate directly in the dasher's exploits. The once-fashionable young man who set out to encounter "Life" has become the contemplative observer.

The gentlemanly roughhouse and coarseness of *Real Life in London* reappears in lower middle-class forms in *Pickwick Papers* and Albert Smith's *The Natural History of the Gent.* While Dickens was the first student of the "gent" phenomenon, Smith was the first to give the swaggering, overdressed, jaunty London adolescents a name. He points out that the gent's object is "to assume a position which he conceives to be superior to his own."[45] This "futile apeing of superiority"[46] involves dress and life-style: the gent, as Ellen Moers has observed, was primarily known for his love of cheap finery and for his equal devotion to pursuits that he considered "swell"—theaters, drinking sprees, the pleasures of the races and the seaside. Professor Moers sums up the gent's major characteristics:

> The Gent was a creature of once-a-month sprees and splurges, of false fronts to calico shirts, of phony jewelry, half-price tickets to the theatre, greasy hair and dirty ears.[47]

He was an outsider looking in at the genteel world of "great fun," at the London pleasures that he could hardly afford. Like the dasher, he was unpolished; his "coarse annoying gallantry" to an approaching girl represents his lack of manners. Gents were fond of "puffing smoke into every bonnet they met."[48] The gent was ostentatious, raucous, impecunious, and vulgar; his manners were bad and his origins were usually questionable. He was no gentleman on several counts, but he aped dashers and men of fashion with a style that was atrocious—yet full of brio.

In *Pickwick Papers* Dickens pioneered the analysis of this essentially Regency social type and gave Albert Smith paradigms for his gents in Ben Allen and Bob Sawyer, two medical students. Mr. Pickwick's first impressions of the young men are ironic in the light of what the two are really like: "very fine fellows with judgements matured by observation and reflection; tastes refined by reading and study." They are anything but: Ben is a coarse fellow who wears no collar:

> Bob had about him that sort of slovenly smartness, and swaggering gait, which is peculiar to young gentlemen who smoke in the streets by day, and shout and scream in the same by night, call waiters by their Christian names, and do various other acts and deeds of an equally facetious description.

At the dinner table, they talk about brandy, cigars, and pork chops in one breath; a moment later they start discussing the dissection of a muscular child's leg. Mr. Pickwick attempts to stop their disgusting dialogue. Yet this swagger and lack of good manners paradoxically goes along with a desire for genteel display and a keeping up of appearances. Bob's party at his Lant Street rooming house is the quintessence of gentism: grubby hospitality overlaid with a few gentlemanly amenities. Bob gives orders to the servant girl as though he were master of a household rather than a boarder whose rent is overdue. He is a member of the servant-keeping classes, if only for the evening. His "desperate sternness" in ordering hot water for the brandy is a pathetic attempt to remain master of the situation. No one, however, will listen to a poor medical student, and the evening culminates with the guests being thrown out by the landlady and referred to as "brutes" for their boisterousness.

If all this seems silly, rather pathetic and futile, it might be appropriate to end a discussion of enjoyment with the disillusioned words of Lord Chesterfield—perhaps the most cutting commentator on the nature of gentlemanly pleasures:

> I have run the silly rounds of pleasure, and have done with them all. I have enjoyed all the pleasures of the world: I appraise them at their real worth, which is, in truth, very low. Those who have only seen their outside always overrate them, but I have been behind the scenes, I have seen all the coarse pulleys and dirty ropes which move their gaudy machines, and I have also seen and smelt the tallow candles which illuminate the whole decoration, to the astonishment and admiration of the ignorant audience. When I reflect on what I have seen, what I have heard, and what I have done, I can hardly persuade myself that all that frivolous hurry and bustle and pleasure in the world had any reality; but I look upon all that is past as one of those romantic dreams which opium commonly occasions, and I do by no means desire to repeat the nauseous dose.[49]

CONCLUSION

RESENTMENTS AND REDISCOVERIES— FORSTER, LAWRENCE, AND OTHER MODERNS

THE DISDAIN that Lord Chesterfield felt for futile pleasure is one among many negative responses that have crowded the pages of literature and influenced the lives of people in the last two centuries. Following the French Revolution, an avalanche of criticism and misfortune descended on the gentleman: the savage indictment of Dickens, the scathing analyses of the landed interest in the philosophy of Jeremy Bentham and John Stuart Mill, and the anger of Carlyle at do-nothing aristocrats were some of the most brilliant assaults. The brightest and the best—writers, intellectuals, reformers—have found the ideal and the reality of gentry life sorely wanting in sense and human value.

In our own time creative writers as well as thinkers have offered both direct and oblique attacks on power and privilege. Describing the forms that such opposition has taken would constitute a whole study of antitraditionalism. Our purpose is rather to indicate what these lines of resentment are: how several representative writers followed up on the criticism of earlier centuries. And once we have determined the variety of negative response, the final question remains: does the gentleman as an ideal have any chance of survival? Are people today likely to be drawn to any of the more attractive and socially useful features of gentlemanly life?

E. M. Forster's novels often exhibit the least attractive features of modern gentility. Those who are born to wealth and some amount of privilege are in danger of falling short of a reasonable standard of human kindliness and social decency. Sensitive genteel people also exist in his work, but they are likely to be thwarted in trying to express their better instincts by those in their status group. In *The Longest Journey* and *Howards End,* people of fine feeling and conscience face a hostile world of convention and genteel recklessness or indifference; in attempting to live vitally or to be socially useful, they are resisted at every turn—and, in several instances, they are destroyed. Rickie Elliot, the artistic young man whose struggle is expressed in the title of *The Longest Journey,* is twice in his life at the mercy of gentlemen: as a boy with a club foot, he has first been taunted by his dignified and coldly mocking father and then been abused at a public school by hearty types who love games and group spirit. When he grows up, he ironically thinks that "civilization" will protect him from gentlemanly muscularity. But his own errors in judgment lead him once again into the camp of the genteel bullies. Searching for emotional satisfaction and love, he allows himself to be taken over by Agnes Pembroke, a strong-willed, worldly, seductive woman whose ambition is to shape him—the abstracted artist—into the mold of the successful competitor. Agnes's brother Herbert, a stupid philistine who is getting a reputation as a house master at a second-rate public school, draws Rickie into his world of boosterism, bullying, and hypocrisy. (Herbert spends time in propping him up, making sure that he follows the orthodox line.) Rickie becomes a schoolmaster and outdoes everyone in the role of classroom martinet and enemy of the poor day boys from the village of Sawston. Once a cultivated and decent Cambridge man with artistic aspirations, he has been twisted into a shape not unlike that of his father.

The book's central conflict turns on a question of gentlemanly character versus rational intelligence and emotional openness. The first force is represented by Sawston School and Herbert. Forster injects considerable irony into Herbert's description of the Sawston ideal: a man who "shoots straight and hits straight and speaks straight" and who "has the instincts of a Christian and a gentleman." The reader receives this declaration as so much cant and hot air in light of Herbert's machinations. Sawston—once an old grammar school intended for local boys—is on its way to becoming a snooty, undistinguished copy of the great public schools. Its rise represents anything but "shooting straight"; its ideals—rigid organization, playing the game, stamping out individuality, discouraging reflection—are a mockery of humanistic education and express the worst aspects of late nineteenth-century public-school exclusivism. Forster parodies familiar rhetoric about the public schools as preparation for the real world by having Pembroke speak of Sawston as "the world in miniature." Indeed, it is not; it only replicates on a small scale the violence and injustice of a hierarchical society untempered by reason and feeling.

Intelligence in the novel is a distinctly ungentlemanly quality. It is best represented by Rickie's Cambridge friend, Stewart Ansell, an aspiring philosopher who sizes up the conventional Agnes on first meeting and ignores her. He is no gentleman, as Rickie says; yet he is rich in insight and warmth. The son of a distinctly ungenteel retail businessman from a small town, Ansell is far enough from the Sawston set to appraise what is happening to his friend; he watches as Rickie descends into the depths of inauthenticity and personal confusion. His great moment in the novel comes when he visits Sawston and makes a scene by telling Rickie the truth about the Elliot family connections. Earlier on in the book, Forster has introduced a rather loutish, bawdy young man named Stephen Wonham, a hanger-on at Cadover, the estate of Rickie's rich aunt. Rickie, already under the spell of Agnes's gentility, recoils from this unsavory fellow only to learn that he is his half brother (presumably his father's bastard). In the explosive scene at Sawston, Ansell tells the real story. Stephen is the son of Rickie's mother by a local farmer; he is a rather unsubtly drawn romantic child of the Wiltshire soil, a noble savage with a foul mouth and a good heart. Rickie comes to love him as his mother's son, but also, in true gentlemanly fashion, tries to make him into something finer than he is. Pursuing the unreal—in this case another illusion about people—Rickie meets his end in trying to drag his dead-drunk brother from a railroad track. Forster's resolution—high melodrama mixed with reflection about the future of England—leaves Stephen and his child to represent the new England.

> Though he could not phrase it, he believed that he had guided the future of our race, and that century after century, his thoughts and passions would triumph in England.

Thoughts and passions, as we have learned from Dickens's Mrs. General, are decidedly ungenteel: E. M. Forster makes a point of showing how the conventional gentle people of his era can no more come to terms with heart and intellect than the properly genteel characters in *Little Dorrit*. *Howards End*, Forster's masterful study of failures in human connection, essentially takes up the major question of gentlemanly responsibility. Once a settled issue in the pages of the de Coverley papers, the whole area of duty and responsiveness became a key issue in Victorian novels that dealt with social neglect. Forster gives a post–World War I account of what it means to be genteel and to fail at the humane enterprise of learning about one's fellow man and caring about him. The novel is rich in its accountings of how the privileged live in emotional ignorance. In studying three groups in the vast middle class—the intellectuals, the prosperous business people, and the white-collar wage slaves—Forster shows how connections can only be forceably or tragically established: people in his world can only be brought to accept each other when they are plunged into disaster or when they are thrown together by circumstances. The Schlegel sisters, two intellectuals living off family money in a comfortable London house with their gentlemanly and languorous brother Tibby, are Forster's portraits of the new people of moral sensitivity: bred up on enlightened social ideals, democratic ideas, and distrust of profit and birth, they are prototypical modern people of intelligence and conscience; they can be found in the great cities of Western Europe and America—and their voices have been clearly heard on every public issue. Forster makes them appealing, well-meaning, cultured—but not altogether successful in grappling with the real world of poverty, power, and bad will. One sister, Helen, is briefly attracted to Mr. Wilcox's son—and this connection sets the novel's plot in motion: the book is about how both groups, the intellectuals and the commercial types, somehow fail in their relations with the struggling working people in modern London. The Schlegels meet Leonard Bast, an insurance-company clerk, and as he is drawn into their world, he moves toward his tragic end. Leonard is a modern yearner, not altogether unlike poor boys in nineteenth-century novels who seek culture and some degree of refinement while pursuing their seedy urban lives. He reads Ruskin while living in a cramped flat with his vulgar, pathetic wife, Jackie. In a marvelously ironic scene, the Schlegels steal Leonard's umbrella by accident; later they give understanding—and Helen sleeps with him out of sympathy. But what Leonard gets is less important than what is taken from him. Mr. Wilcox, it turns out, once had Jackie as his mistress; Wilcox also irresponsibly passes on a bad tip about a job that causes Leonard to become one of London's unemployed; as if that is not enough, England's privileged—in this case Charles Wilcox—take up the sword against the poor fellow. In a spectacularly dramatic scene, Charles punishes Leonard for getting Helen Schlegel pregnant—he slaps him with the flat of a sword. Leonard dies of heart failure, the victim of a stupid gentleman's attempt to defend honor.

The Wilcoxes and the Schlegels, the materialists and the idealists, are the inheritors of the gentleman's function: the first want no part of duty, but love power; the second fear power, but still hold to the idea of social responsibility. Between them, they destroy a young man and in so doing ironically act out a twentieth-century fable of genteel failure: all that is left at the end is a ruined Wilcox—finally connected with his idealistic in-laws because of the tragedy of his son's conviction for manslaughter—and Helen's little classless child, a baby who will inherit a small country house that will be nothing like a gentleman's seat.

The genteel middle class in *Howards End* is also at odds with itself. The intellectuals like Helen Schlegel see the Wilcox family power as "a fraud, just a wall of newspapers and motor-cars and golf-clubs"; there is nothing behind it but "panic and emptiness." (Forster's persona concurs and says the Wilcoxes depart from their rented country place "leaving a little dust and a little money behind.") Margaret and Helen's world of good manners and progressive ideals is also quite separated from the high-handed vulgarity of the Wilcoxes: the latter are the type of people who insult an old woman at Howards End who gives a wedding present beyond her means. They send the gift back to the store, and thereafter the woman hates the family that injured her pride. For their part, the Wilcoxes cannot understand the sensitivities of the Schlegels: the former think the lower classes should vaporize socially, yet continue to produce wealth for their betters. Forster's England in *Howards End* is a sustained view of a country blasted by the failed intentions and indifference of two kinds of middle-class genteel people.

The lines of resentment in *Howards End* are complicated, but essentially a matter of Forster's confrontation with the tragic limits of ideals and material prosperity. Lionel Trilling called the book "a work of full responsibility,"[1] principally because it looks squarely at the disorder and lack of connection created in modern England by the intelligent and the comfortable. The collapse of the Wilcox-Schlegel world is no accident of fate.

More problematic in his attitude toward privilege and power, D. H. Lawrence offers a rather ambivalent treatment of the gentleman and his ideals in *Lady Chatterley's Lover*. The most prominent social feature of the book is its heavy-handed attack directed at Sir Clifford Chatterley and his life as the impotent, but brutal pseudosquire of Wragby, his estate. Instead of being a protector of his dependents, Sir Clifford is a genteel profiteer, the owner of mines and the exploiter of a downtrodden and rather surly village of proletarians. There was "no communication between Wragby Hall and Tebershall village": "No caps were touched, no curtseys bobbed." Like the relationship between the poor Basts and the rich Wilcoxes in *Howards Ends,* Clifford and his colliers are connected only through dislike: "Gulf impassable, and a quiet resentment on either side." Sir Clifford thinks of his employees—like Nero's slaves or Ford's factory workers—as not quite human. A person who is "inwardly hard and separate," Chatterley becomes the ruthless and impotent symbol of the new order of England. His wife Connie thinks of him as a "dead fish of a gentleman with his celluloid soul!" Lawrence heaps abuse on him—his heartless intellectualism, his love of literary successes, and his inability to communicate sexually or emotionally are his greatest sins. One of the more obvious aspects of Lawrence's indictment involves Sir Clifford's lack of consideration. In a scene in which the baronet's wheelchair breaks down near the woods, Mellors the gamekeeper is rudely enlisted to push the cripple along the path; this is taxing for Mellors since he has had pneumonia. Later that day, Connie upbraids her husband for his crude and inconsiderate treatment of his employee. The want of common sympathy in Chatterley makes her say, "Why my father is ten times the human being you are: you *gentleman!*" Fixing the precise nature of Lawrence's resentment is not easy: Connie's remark, after all, has a certain ambiguous quality, especially in light of what later comes out about the gentleman. It may simply be sarcasm: So that's what a gentleman is! Or it might mean: And you consider yourself a gentleman! The reader of *Lady Chatterley's Lover* is likely to wonder about this further when he sees some of her references to born gentlemen and to Mellors. Sir Malcolm Reid, Connie's father, is unquestionably a man of birth and a typical hearty, pleasure-loving member of the landed gentry, but he gets off unscathed by Lawrence's savage social criticism because he is an openhearted, plainspoken, latter-day barbarian of the Squire Western sort. He and Mellors get together at a club to discuss the affair between gamekeeper and gentlewoman. The father, untouched by Christian morality, is as bluff and jolly about the whole thing as the most unreconstructed gentleman of the fox-hunting and shooting set. Nothing to feel except happiness at his daughter's sexual satisfaction; nothing to fear but the man of blood's nemesis—scandal. For Lawrence, being a gentleman is not so bad a thing so long as one is not a neutered, modernized snob involved with capitalist profit in mining. But once a man has lost his feeling for the physical world and for the hearts of his fellow creatures, he is to be condemned. It is also interesting (and rather perplexing) to note that Lawrence goes easy on Sir Leslie Winter, a relative of Sir Clifford's and master of Shipley, an exquisite neoclassical estate; this elderly man is the obverse side of Sir Malcolm—not a robust barbarian, but a fine gentleman of the eighteenth-century type, complete with patent leather pumps, purple socks, and a nonchalant attitude toward the world around him. The irony that is directed on him is far less excoriating than that directed on Chatterley. Shipley is totally dependent on the colliers' labors, and Sir Leslie—good worldling that he is—lets them traipse through parts of his park, litter the ornamental ponds, and scowl at him. While he doesn't take his evening stroll for fear of them, he still feels that they are better than the deer that once roamed the park: they make money for him. For all the satiric bite of this portrait, Lawrence's indictment is not delivered in the lathered-up rhetoric he uses on Sir Clifford. After all, this man loves pleasure.

The complications in Lawrence's resentment do not end with men of birth and privilege. Mellors the gamekeeper was the outrage of 1928 because of his phallic consciousness; today he comes across as something of a mystery because of the ideal that his actions and bearing represent. His social identity is muddled by all sorts of circumstances. A local working-class boy, he distinguished himself at the Sheffield Grammar School; he served in the army in India as an officer and returned to England only to be consigned (although not apparently resigned) to the subservient role of gamekeeper. Along the way he has acquired a perfect command of the King's English while stubbornly maintaining a broad, almost comic Derbyshire accent on certain occasions. Standard English is for intelligent discussion and routine social life; Derbyshire is for intimacy and angry response. He can discuss books and ideas, but he can also lapse into crudity and rudeness. He is tender and gentle and kind—and also coarse and domineering as he rhapsodizes about Connie's anatomy. In some ways he is a social centaur—half frank-spoken, openhearted gentleman and half resentful proletarian.[2] In appearance, as Connie reminds her father, he is thoroughly "presentable"; no local lout or clodhopper, he has the bearing of a gentleman. But he can be as boorish as Walter Morel in *Sons and Lovers* when he is roused to anger by Connie's conventional sister Hilda.

His origins in the history of the gentleman as an ideal can be traced to areas that we have explored. His self-possession and fierce independence of public opinion are actually characteristic of the man of blood. His gentleness, capacity for human sympathy, and unfailing decency as a person lead us back to the Victorian ideal of the man of fine feeling and simple origins. Mellors at times seems like Dickens's Joe Gargery with sexual organs attached. Like Joe he is a man of delicate feeling who suffers because of the snobbery around him: he is helpful and tender and capable of living with dignity despite the degrading circumstances at Wragby. Like Joe Gargery, he endures. Lawrence reinvents the Victorian ideal of the man of gentle spirit by conceiving of sexual tenderness and virility as the hallmarks of the true gentleman. His resentment of the gentleman does not prevent him from fabricating his own preeminent man.

Twentieth-century literary protest against the world of blood and privilege is usually not a matter of geniuses like Forster and Lawrence and their analyses of a damaged ideal. Distinguished lesser novelists and thinkers in other fields have expressed important resentments that add to the dissolution of earlier ideals and also present new versions of excellence. At odds with tradition, they offer intimacy or authenticity or material well-being in place of the gentleman's code of honor. Intellectuals, morally conscientious people, successful professionals and business people, artists, angry proletarians, and even gentry people themselves, have rebelled against the models of gentility presented in this book and substituted their own ideals of dignity and worth.

One significant blow struck against the gentleman came from another aristocracy—the British intellectual elite of the late nineteenth and early twentieth century. This group—a fairly cohesive class whose activities have been studied by Lionel Trilling, Noel Annan, E. M. Forster, Paul Levy, and John Maynard Keynes[3]—sometimes overlaps in its origins with the gentry, but also has a great many members who trace their family roots to proud middle-class business and professional people in the early nineteenth century. The members are often distinguished from the gentry by an ethos of achievement, hard work, and occupational dignity. And yet some of their characteristics are not unlike those of the gentry: Paul Levy remarks that one was (and some still are) born into it,[4] and its members possessed the self-confidence usually associated with aristocrats. The nineteenth-century members included Darwins, Wedgwoods, Thorntons, Stephens, Trevelyans, Macaulays—men of intellect, generally educated at Cambridge University, who stood somewhat apart from the gentleman of birth and privilege whom we have discussed.

G. E. Moore, the philosopher whose work in ethics had wide-ranging consequences for English life and thought, was part of this group: the son of a well-read doctor who was a dissenter, Moore was brought up on a code of rigorous intellectual activity and devotion to knowledge that set him apart from typical gentlemen of the monied classes. At Cambridge he was asked to join the Apostles, a secret society devoted to debating questions of philosophical and artistic interest; this exclusive group—its membership consisted of some of the most brilliant men of the nineteenth century, especially those who attained high distinction at Cambridge—was something quite different from the clubs and societies devoted to socializing, social consolidation of one's class position, and exclusion of middle-class men of doubtful background. (In *After Long Silence,* Michael Straight has quoted a friend's remark that to be an Apostle one had to be *"very* brilliant" and *"extremely* nice.") Its members—while usually comfortably middle class or better—were quite unconcerned with good society and fine living as the gentleman would understand them. Its meetings included coffee and endless witty and brilliant talk: typically a session was shaped around a presentation of a paper by a member. Moore's own thought was nurtured in this elite but not consciously genteel setting. In his time the Apostles usually discussed subjects that tended to erode the gentlemanly consensus—women's suffrage, free love, modern aesthetics, radical reform. Moore became one of the century's most brilliant Apostles when he published *Principia Ethica,* a work that was misunderstood and selectively read in an influential way.[5] A complex consideration of duty and "good," the work was received by the Cambridge set of young men as a modernist manifesto about the good life. While the Victorian code of living well was some form of the gentleman's code—being a fine gentleman or a Christian gentleman or an old-fashioned squire or a public school man or a man of gentle feelings—the twentieth-century intellectual code that emanated from Cambridge was a loose adaptation of certain points in Moore's great work. One interpreter of Moore's influence on the young men of his generation selects three ideas that were of special significance.[6] The first held that goodness—so much a part of the gentleman's code in the eighteenth and nineteenth century—could not be defined. The second involved the championing of "states of mind" as opposed to codes of behavior: "By far the most valuable things, which we know or can imagine, are certain states of consciousness, which may be roughly described as the pleasures of human intercourse and the enjoyment of beautiful objects." The third isolates Moore's complex idea about duty: that the rightness of an action cannot easily be calculated and comes from the not easily foreseeable character of its consequences.

Moore's "states of mind," his most influential idea, effectively destroys the gentleman's world of self-assertion, consumption, and display. A matter of consciousness and the cultivation of emotions, this idea of the good life moves "the ideal" away from pride in family, possessions, socially correct education, social duty, and pleasure of the worldly sort. Moore's "enjoyment" is the fine-tuned response of the person whose life is directed toward friendship and contemplation of beauty—not toward power relationships and display. As for his idea about what "duty" is, there is little chance of linking the gentleman's straightforward paternalistic community service to Moore's skeptical notions about what is right. Moore feels that duty is not a universal and right actions are dependent on the nature of one's society. Such a relativistic view of responsibility is quite apart from the gentry's tradition of helping people by offering example and demanding obedience. Moore's ethical person is going in a different direction from the public-spirited gentlemen we have discussed. His "ideal" of living well and doing right is infinitely more complicated than the gentleman's rough-and-ready prescription for leadership, a prescription based on the notion that wellborn people should set a tone and command respect. Moore's way of looking at the world established a modernist perspective that was adopted by the Bloomsbury intellectuals and that has even been traced to Guy Burgess, the British mole who betrayed his country in the interests of a larger conception of duty.[7] The Cambridge gentleman Communist is one of the most complicated variations of and departures from the traditional ideal. Retaining, like Burgess, his love of Eton, his old school ties, and his personal decorum, he nevertheless discards his honor as an Englishman by spying and defecting to Moscow. Can one be a gentleman and a Communist agent? Yes and no. Culturally and socially, Burgess had the indelible stamps of the gentleman; yet betrayal of the realm violated the idea of the gentleman's obligation to protect and perpetuate the English social order.[8]

The teleplay by Alan Bennett on Burgess, called *An Englishman Abroad,* is an ironic exploration of the mutifaceted spy: scamp and liar, trickster and betrayer, Burgess is the man who ratted on his kind—and at the same time remained loyal to their folkways, tastes, and behavior. He emerges as a rather sympathetic figure who still has a caring heart and a charming manner. And he did what he did, we are reminded, from a sense of duty. Monstrous as it may seem to many, his nature is that of the gentleman as anticonventionalist. In Moscow he misses his tailor, the Reform Club, and the gossip of his peers—all the while defending the Soviet system.

Attacks on gentlemanly life-style and power in our century have been relentless. Our purpose is to categorize types rather than study the process decade by decade. Forster and Lawrence attacked the gentleman's heart (or lack of it), offering vitalism in place of convention.

Moore cut the ethical certainties from under the gentleman and offered the subtleties of consciousness in place of bold self-assertion. A few less famous writers have dealt serious blows to the gentleman's position. Simon Raven, a London writer whose book *The English Gentleman* explains the decline of the ideal, offers both indictments and predictions about new social forms to displace the traditional gentleman. Raven presents himself as a rueful escapee from the ideal of gentlemanly conduct, a former Charterhouse student (expelled for "the usual reason," i.e., homosexuality) and King's College man who wants to confess to irresponsibility and dishonesty while at the same time pointing to the deficiencies of the standard he has fallen short of.[9] Raven's personal story, an ironic tale of degeneration and betrayal of trust at school and in adult life, is about his failure to adopt the values of Charterhouse.

The book essentially sorts out two ways of looking at the world: the gentleman's view that he owes something to his society and the upper-class person's notion that privilege and pleasure do not carry with them any obligations. In tracing his own emergence as a member of the upper class, Raven also follows England's abandonment of the gentleman standard: the personal narrative is complemented by a treatment of prototypical contemporary types and situations—people who are prosperous London swingers and media personalities of the late fifties in scenes where they betray the ideal of the traditional landed classes. "The Scavengers," modish snobs and sycophants, are contrasted with the ideal-type gentry—especially with one Matthew Tench, an honest and considerate country gentleman and army officer who wanted to do his duty and whose world of assumed privilege and modest display is ruined by World War I and the rise of rich men in search of personal gain. Tench is also the victim of taxes and democracy: by World War II he is reduced to selling his estate and enjoying his occasional bottle of good wine. Such types are regarded by the populace as "the class enemy with the haw-haw voice"; meanwhile a group of vulgar go-getters and sharp dealers—not unlike Forster's Charles Wilcox who also had no sense of community obligation—are taking over.

Raven's point about all this is that England is headed for an ugly future unless some type other than the upper-class man can be located. Almost like Carlyle's search for new aristocracies, Raven's argument becomes an attempt to present a credible authority to take the place of the gentleman. Each observer of English life will have to decide for himself about Raven's description of a new code, that of the person whose authority is derived from learning, skepticism, tolerance, and frankness. The type discovered by Raven is none other than—you guessed it—the intellectuals at King's College, Cambridge. Such people, we are told, are a kind of last best hope. They are not dogmatic like the gentleman; their delicate, deliberative, and intelligent approach to the problem of guiding others is quite different from the gentleman's self-righteous attitudes. Raven explains at considerable length how he himself—a rather caddish, dishonest, irresponsible fellow—submitted to their law. The dons at King's had rules about using college facilities; when Raven broke the rules, he was punished by a genial but firm authority. Standards of intellectual honesty, logic, and decency were held up by the dons, and the students respected them. A new kind of deference society was formed—that is, if the observer is willing to believe that these authorities are something entirely different from the man of good breeding and consideration. I, for one, am inclined to think that this civilized form of authority is an updating of the gentleman's code of honor: just as the dueling classes once thought honor was repute and the Christian gentleman thought it was honesty and purity, so the intellectuals have rehabilitated the ideal and made it into reason and common decency. Raven even admits that he is searching for a way that gentlemanly courtesy can be fed into a new kind of leadership.

The responses of Raven's *The English Gentleman* to the problem of duty and the ideals of the good are not disconsonant with G. E. Moore's skepticism and championing of states of consciousness. Raven, like Moore, is in pursuit of a subtle idea of social responsibility that goes beyond the gentleman's flat-footed paternalism; he is also pursuing ideals of intellectual community and an appreciation of beauty that are far more complex than the gentlemanly pleasures that we have outlined earlier.

Other writers who have found the gentleman and gentility lacking have not been at such pains to adumbrate new forms of preeminence. Their criticisms of tradition and conventions have concentrated on reducing the ideal or blasting it with irony or presenting it as Raven's upper-class greed and exclusivism. Laura Talbot, author of a 1952 minor classic called *The Gentlewomen,* reviews some familiar territory with acerbic wit and a certain despair. Her book is set in World War II England and concentrates on the warped character and values of Miss Bolby, a governess obsessed with gentility. While not strictly speaking about the gentleman, the novel becomes the occasion for surveying what has happened to the gentleman's way of life and attitudes. Talbot, a scion of a noble family herself, observes her character, Miss Bolby, making a fool of herself as the governess to Lord Rushford's children. The technique of the novel—basically the ploy of reducing genteel usages to the caricature level—involves Miss Bolby's observation of the proprieties that better-born people are careless about or a bit ashamed of in the modern world. The daughter of respectable and genteel middle-class parents and the sister of a woman who has married into the higher reaches of the gentry, Miss Bolby lives a life devoted to keeping the children in her charge (and the grown-ups) up to the genteel mark. Like Dickens's Mrs. General in *Little Dorrit,* she never quite finds the real world refined enough; her style, the euphemism and the evasion, is a matter of calling her former boardinghouse a pied-à-terre and correcting the children's idioms. The true gentlefolk—Lord Rushford, his wife, the suffering children of their two marriages, and some neighbors—are rather frank, plain-spoken people who take manners for granted. Lord and Lady Rushford's aristocratic neighbors are anything but genteel in Miss Bolby's terms. Lord and Lady Archie Meredith, an old couple staying with Meredith's brother, Lord Corwen, are a rough-and-ready pair of country types who seem like the lineal descendants of Fielding's characters; Lady Archie, it turns out, once had an affair with Miss Bolby's sister's husband; she is anything but Victorian in her sexual attitudes. Frank references to the affair on the part of the Rushfords enrage Miss Bolby: she even goes so far as to accuse Lord Rutherford, her employer, of "effrontery" in asking her to sing before Lady Archie and the company. Deeply disturbed by the gossip and the supposed stain on the Bolby family honor, Miss Bolby spends the rest of the novel trying to maintain her position by high-hatting her betters.

While the middle-class snob Miss Bolby asserts herself, the highborn people pretty much ignore her or brush her off. Lord Corwen, a dotty bird fancier with an expensive aviary, is the one exception: the old lecher sees a good-looking woman and in his bumbling way tries to attract her. But the wellborn people and Miss Bolby seem to be moving in different directions in Talbot's plot: after a tragic incident involving the secretary Miss Pickford—a woman killed in an auto accident after being abused by Miss Bolby—the tenure of Miss Bolby concludes. She returns to her pied-à-terre, sends flirtatious notes to Lord Corwen, but is ignored. Talbot's biting narrative seems to resolve itself as the force of gentility is casually repelled by both the modern aristocrats and the circumstances of their world. No one quite cares that the Miss Bolbys of England are alive—this in a novel that concentrates so much attention on her petty snobbery. Lord Rushford is a matter-of-fact, practical man who loves his estate but warns one of his children against romantic illusions of grandeur: "Those days are over. It's no good growing up with that sort of idea." As the novel ends, Miss Bolby is the only one left who treasures the idea.

Such illusions and breakdowns of the genteel world are also central to Philip Larkin's distinguished wartime novel *Jill.* Its protagonist, John Kemp, is a working-class boy who makes it to Oxford on scholarship; the narrative is about the way that the styles and attractions of the gentleman excite him, cause him to fantasize, and finally land him in a state of disillusionment not unlike that of Pip in *Great Expectations.* The plot of the book is curiously similar to Dickens's fable of working-class innocence and genteel experience. Like Pip, John comes from the provinces to the great world, works through his crazed dream about a genteel woman, and emerges (after an illness like Pip's) with a better understanding of the falsity of the gentlemanly code. When John gets to Oxford, he finds that his snobbish, rather vulgar roommate Christopher has a supercilious attitude toward this young man from up north; in order to secure some prestige for himself, John invents a "sister" named Jill, a boarding-school girl to whom he begins to write long letters. Gradually the fictional character—like Pip's distorted vision of Estella—comes to occupy a significant place in his daily life. And one day he sees a real-life equivalent of Jill on an Oxford street. After he tracks her down, he receives an ironic jolt; the beautiful young girl is a cousin of a woman in his roommate's set. When John tries to have a tea date with the girl, the older cousin scotches it; when he persists and accosts the girl at a party, Christopher steps in and knocks him down; a jolly group of the better people at college throw John into the quad fountain. As the novel ends, John is getting over pneumonia as well as taking stock of his damaged career at the university. Meanwhile, the caddish Christopher and his girlfriend Elizabeth are off to London and ready to begin a coldly calculated affair. The final scene has a small dog, an outsider from the street, growling at Elizabeth.

The tension of John's romance and the intelligence of the novel's vision prevent the plot from degenerating into a cautionary tale about nice working-class intellectuals and nasty gentlemen. The intensity of John's feelings for his own fabrication also makes the book quite ironic: as we move along with John's strategies to find Jill and to impress his better-born friends, we move into a dizzy and ultimately destructive realm. Larkin's distance from John is delicately maintained: we sympathize with him and see that the Oxford swells are cold, foulmouthed, prurient, dishonest, and lazy; but we also see that he has fallen prey to the all-too-available illusions of Oxford life. As John is betrayed, we have the sense that he has taken part in his own downfall. Larkin's narrative is another resentful version of what has happened to the luminous ideal of gentlemanly life: it has all become a matter of caddish rich people victimizing confused newcomers.

The variety of negative responses to the gentleman that we have presented is not intended to convey the sense that the ideal is entirely dissolved: although the antigentlemanly tendencies in our century are stronger than the progentleman forces, they have not entirely swept the field. Fictional characters of good family, good manners, and honest instincts have played a significant, but minor role in modern literature. Evelyn Waugh, Joseph Conrad, Ford Madox Ford, and Graham Greene are a few novelists who have kept the ideal alive—while showing the brutal competition it receives from the modern economy, the state, the professional classes, and the rich. Gentlemen usually are losers in modern fiction—typically Lord Sebastian Flyte, the drunken charmer of *Brideshead Revisited,* is destroyed while the vulgar Rex Motram does quite well.

The gentleman is most successful not as a durable ideal and model, but as a popular entertainment. "No one can say that in the 1980s the gentleman is a social force," Philip Mason observes.[10] Yet, he has become a media event in *Brideshead Revisited;* in the 1970s his life-style became an overwhelmingly popular item on the television series *Upstairs, Downstairs.* The film *Chariots of Fire* is animated in part by the conflict between a professional athlete and the reactionary forces of Cambridge University: one of the best scenes shows the ambitions of an inspired runner pitted against the snobbery of the master of Caius College. The public, it should be noted, was drawn to the style of the movie and to the struggle within an essentially gentlemanly world. Today the gentleman is a delightful image, the focus of exhibitions, art books, serials, and even some serious criticism. Although the power of the landed gentry did not outlive World War I—and was severely curtailed as far back as the 1870s with the failure of the harvests and the growing importance of American agriculture in the world economy—the mystique of the great houses is very much alive in the popular imagination; while no longer a force for social cohesion, the landed estate is an aesthetic object, a source of pleasure and instruction for the public, a "treasure." On both sides of the Atlantic—witness the "Treasures of Britain" at the National Gallery in Washington—people have an insatiable appetite for the gentry's artifacts. The gentleman's house is now a public spectacle available to many thousands—either through visits or through television programming. The aristocratic estate is so popular that it even makes for a good setting for a Schweppes tonic commercial: and on top of that, the Lord who is produced in the ad has refreshing politeness. Anyone taking a genteel inventory in the 1980s is bound to have a long list of such items that endure as reminders of the gentleman's past.

Some of the best reminders in our time are good books about the life-style, morality, and ethos of the gentleman. Richard Gill's *Happy Rural Seat* concentrates on the representation of the country house in modern fiction and demonstrates how the gentleman's residence has been depicted as both a principle of coherence and an emblem of in-justice in our century.[11] Gill himself colors the book with his own sensitive attitude toward the house as social institution and contrasts the houses with the ominous forces of modern self-absorption and isolation. Shirley Letwin's *The Gentleman in Trollope* spends its time "explicating the morality that defines the gentleman" according to one novelist: as she analyzes the humanistic strain in the gentleman, Letwin de-emphasizes ideas of birth and status that we have examined. Such an approach—questionable because of the traditional concern with pedigree in so many English writers[12]—is nevertheless a sign of our own times: a good critic sees permanent moral value in an outdated social type.

A. N. Wilson, a prolific young novelist, sees a different kind of use in the characteristics of the gentleman: in his ironic book *Gentlemen in England: A Vision* he uses various kinds of gentlemen—the aged Regency man of taste, the sober Victorian professional, the not-quite-genteel artist, the man of pleasure—to form a collective picture of mid-Victorian England; in showing the reader how each of these types acts in relationship to a young girl, Wilson gives us versions of gentility that seem to have significance for our own age as well as for his fabricated Victorians. The behavior, instincts, manners, and speech of his people are meant to remind us that, although they talk about the Oxford Movement and worry about proprieties, they are not antediluvian. Wilson's gentlemen are alive and comically accessible to us as we watch them seeking sexual gratification or professional achievement or social distinction.

Working as an art critic and cultural historian, Mark Girouard has written two very valuable books that focus on country-house architecture and one other excellent volume that deals with the adaptation of the chivalric ideal in the nineteenth and twentieth century. The architecture books—*Life in the English Country House* and *The Victorian Country House*—are sumptuous and detailed presentations of the ways in which houses expressed the gentleman's values and interests. While he leads his readers into the practical and aesthetic aspects of the gentleman's life over a series of centuries in the first volume, he necessarily brings in dismal conclusions about the future of the landed order—and by extension the gentleman's authority in the contemporary world:

> A few owners of country houses are still engaged in running the country or the county, but the old automatic correlation between ownership of an estate and the right to execute power has vanished.[13]

The houses receive "sympathy, visitors, and grants":[14] while this decline in political and social authority does not necessarily mean that the gentleman's moral authority is at an end, it does suggest that such authority is in great danger. Or as he says elsewhere in the book, the gentry has "lost the coherence of an integrated and powerful class."[15] And yet all may not be at an end for the gentleman as an ideal; Girouard's own superb volume on chivalry shows that medieval conceptions of honor and self-assertion were capable of being used by people in the nineteenth century; we have no way of determining whether our own age—in some ways no more sordid than the Victorian era—will find the gentleman's code useful or attractive. Pronouncing the gentleman ideal to be stone dead would be a very reckless response to the fact that it has been under fire. The more suspicious people become of technology, expertise, power expressed through cold cash, the force of the nation state, and the muscle of postindustrial civilization, the more likely it is that they may remember another kind of authority. While the base of gentlemanly power—the country house and the influence that comes from it—seems to be a thing of the past, it is still possible that the better features of the gentleman's life—his sense of duty, his love of diversity, his honesty, his good manners—may find ways of expressing themselves in our culture. Professional service, art and literature, religious observance, civic activity, may well be the new mediums through which certain aspects of the gentlemanly life will survive

If this seems chimerical, if the slippage and loss of credibility seem permanently destructive to all aspects of gentlemanly authority, it is perhaps too bad for modern life. It is true that we will then be done with the "better classes" and their special sense of themselves. The citizen will no longer have to defer to individuals as he seeks guidance or material aid or ideals. But the authority of the state and of large organizations has so far not proven very successful in fulfilling the aspirations of most people. We will not tip our caps but we will fill out forms, correspond with agencies, read their instructions and brochures, and try to tell ourselves that we are less misused and mystified than people in a gentlemanly society.

ENDNOTES

PART ONE

1. THE GENTLEMAN OF BIRTH

1. Hippolyte Taine, *Notes on England* (London: Thames and Hudson, 1957), p. 144.

2. Sir Thomas Smith, *The Commonwealth of England* quoted by Sir James Lawrence, *On the Nobility of the British Gentry* (Paris: A. W. Galignani, 1828), p. 15.

3. Ibid., p. 51.

4. Ibid.

5. J. Horace Round, *Peerage and Pedigree* (London: Nisbet and Co., 1910), p. 313.

6. Quoted from the text of Ball's revolutionary sermon at Blackheath (1381) by Carl Van Doren, *The Oxford Dictionary of Quotations* (London: Oxford University Press, 1941), p. 527b.

7. Felix Markham, *Oxford* (London: Weidenfeld and Nicolson, 1967), p. 20.

8. Lawrence Stone, *The Crisis of the Aristocracy* (London: Oxford University Press, 1967), p. 16.

9. Quoted by Lawrence, p. 38.

10. Ibid.

11. Ibid., p. 43.

12. Shirley Robin Letwin, *The Gentleman in Trollope: Individuality and Moral Conduct* (Cambridge: Harvard University Press, 1982).

13. Lawrence, p. 61.

14. Oswald Barron, "The Gentility of Richard Barker," *The Ancestor,* July, 1902, no. 2, pp. 48–54.

15. Esme Wingfield-Stratford, *The Making of a Gentleman* (London: Williams and Norgate, 1938), pp. 45 and 54.

16. Thorsten Veblen, *The Theory of the Leisure Class* (New York: Mentor, 1953), p. 53.

17. George Sitwell, *The Ancestor,* 1902, pp. 69–70.

18. Sylvia Thrupp, *The Merchant Class of Medieval London* (Ann Arbor: University of Michigan Press, 1961), p. 236.

19. Ibid.

20. Sitwell, p. 69.

21. Ibid.

22. See below, sections 3 and 4, on honor and behavior.

23. Stone, p. 26.

24. Peter Laslett, *The World We Have Lost* (New York: Scribner's, 1965), p. 4.

25. Ibid., p. 20.

26. From Mrs. Alexander's *Hymns for Children* (1848) quoted by Esme Wingfield-Stratford, *The Squire and His Relations* (London: Cassell and Company, Ltd., 1956), p. 313.

27. Quoted by Dorothy George, *Hogarth to Cruikshank: Social Change in Graphic Satire* (New York: Walker, 1967), p. 14.

28. Walter Bagehot, *The English Constitution* (London: Oxford University Press, 1958).

29. Derek Hudson, *Munby: Man of Two Worlds* (New York: Gambit, 1972), p. 73.

30. F. M. L. Thompson, *English Landed Society in the Nineteenth Century* (London: Routledge and Kegan Paul, 1963), p. 3.

31. Edward George Bulwer-Lytton, *England and the English* (London: Bentley, 1933), p. 24.

32. Simon Raven, *The English Gentleman* (London: Anthony Blond, 1961), p. 40.

2. THE GENTLEMAN OF WEALTH

1. Alexis de Tocqueville, *Journey to England and Ireland,* trans. by George Lawrence and K. P. Mayers (New Haven: Yale University Press, 1958), p. 59.

2. Stone, p. 23.

3. Quoted by A. Smythe-Palmer, *The Ideal of a Gentleman or Mirror for Gentlefolks* (London: Routledge, 1908), p. 38.

4. Quoted by Laslett, p. 34.

5. Ruth Kelso, *The Doctrine of the English Gentleman in the Sixteenth Century*

(Urbana, Ill.: University of Illinois Press, 1929), p. 5. See also Stone on "Power," p. 96.

6. Quoted in Laslett, p. 34.

7. See *The Oxford English Dictionary* on the word "gentry."

8. Laslett, pp. 186–187.

9. Tocqueville, p. 17.

10. Ibid., p. 77.

11. Ibid., p. 61.

12. G. K. Chesterton, *The Victorian Age in Literature* (London: Oxford University Press, 1966), p. 9.

13. Stone, p. 20.

14. Tocqueville, p. 67.

15. Quoted by Stone, p. 61.

3. THE GENTLEMAN OF HONOR

1. See Alvin Johnson, ed., *The Encyclopedia of the Social Sciences* (New York: Macmillan, 1930), vol. 7 on "Honor"; also Stone, p. 118 ff.

2. For a treatment of honor as reputation see Henry Fielding, *Jonathan Wild* (New York: Signet Classics, 1961), passim.

3. For early history see J. G. Millingen, *The History of Duelling* (London: Bentley, 1841).

4. Ibid., vol. 1, p. 71. Honor demanded "that the lie was never to be put up with without satisfaction, but by a baseborn fellow."

5. J. Gilchrist, *A Brief Display of the Origin & History of Ordeals* (London: Bulmer and Nicol, 1821, ch. 5.

6. Stone, pp. 113 ff.

7. Millingen, p. 366.

8. Ibid., p. 369.

9. Ibid., p. 370.

10. Ibid., p. 371.

11. Ibid., p. 372.

12. Ibid., p. 373.

13. See Edward Lascelles, *The Life of Charles James Fox* (New York: Octagon, 1970), p. 84. For a parody of all this, see *Pickwick Papers* and the behavior of Dowler, Winkle, Slammer, Mr. Noddy, and Mr. Gunter.

14. Millingen, p. 409.

15. Ibid.

16. J. C. Bluett, *Duelling and the Laws of Honour Explained* (London: Seeley and Burnside, 1835), p. 139.

17. W. L. Burn, *The Age of Equipoise* (New York: Norton, 1965), p. 257.

18. Cited in O. F. Christie, *Transition from Aristocracy, 1832–1867* (London: Seeley, Service & Co., 1922), p. 131.

19. Ibid., p. 134.

20. Burn, p. 259.

21. *The British Code of the Duel* (London: Knight and Lacey, 1924), p. 6.

22. Bluett, p. 89.

23. The term "middle-class gentleman" indeed is a twentieth-century designation: in the process of attempting to describe the nineteenth-century type—the man of honesty and integrity who did not have aristocratic aspirations—we have settled on this term because it indicates the station and life-style of a group of men who were definitely not fashionable and who were content with their place in society.

24. Lionel Trilling, "Mr. Foster's Great Aunt," *A Gathering of Fugitives* (Boston: Beacon Press, 1956), p. 5.

25. Noel Annan, "The Intellectual Aristocracy," *Studies in History,* ed. J. H. Plumb (New York: Longmans, Green, 1955), p. 287.

4. THE GENTLEMAN OF BREEDING

1. Wingfield-Stratford, *The Squire and His Relations,* p. 160.

2. Thomas Babington Macaulay, *The History of England,* ed. Hugh Trevor-Roper (New York: Washington Square Press, 1968), ch. 2.

3. See J. H. Plumb, ed., *Studies in History,* pp. 181–207.

4. Stone, p. 330.

5. E. W. Bovill, *English Country Life* (London: Oxford University Press, 1962), p. 64.

6. Wingfield-Stratford, *The Squire and His Relations,* p. 88.

7. Ibid.

8. Ibid.

9. Ibid.

10. Nimrod (C. J. Apperley), *Memoirs of the Life of the Late John Mytton, Esq.* (London: Kegan Paul, Trench and Trubner, 1834), Part 1.

11. Ibid.

12. J. E. Mason, *Gentlefolk in the Making: Studies in the History of English Courtesy Literature and Related Topics from 1531–1774* (Philadelphia: University of Pennsylvania Press, 1935), p. 2.

13. Ibid., p. 3.

14. Friswell, *The Gentle Life: Essays in Aid of the Formation of Character,* 9th ed. (London: Simpson, Law, 1868), p. 37.

15. A Lady of Rank (C. W. Day), *Hints on Etiquette* (London: Longman, 1861), introduction.

16. Quoted by Wingfield-Stratford, *The Squire and His Relations,* p. 186.

17. Ibid., p. 33.

18. The Chesterfieldian tradition endured well into the nineteenth century, but, alas, there was little of Chesterfield's genius in the writings concerning the behavior of the gentleman. Many such nineteenth-century productions were—in a real sense—travesties of Chesterfield: they were mincing accounts—often written for people of no experience in "good society" (i.e., people who needed to be told how to carry on conversation)—of how to behave with "faultless propriety, perfect harmony, refined simplicity." These catch phrases that recall Chesterfield's doctrines are to be found in *Etiquette for Gentlemen with Hints on the Art of Conversation* (London: Telt and Bogue, 1841). This work, indeed, went through seventeen editions mouthing the following sentiments: "In public, never differ from anybody, nor from anything. The *agreeable* man is one who agrees." The reader is also reminded never to ask a question or never to talk too well.

19. Quoted in Chesterfield, introduction.

20. James Forrester, *The Polite Philosopher* (London: J. Wilson, 1736), p. 5.

21. For a further consideration of Newman's indictment, see below.

22. G. O. Trevelyan, *The Early History of Charles James Fox* (New York: Harper and Brothers, 1901), p. 61.

23. Dorothy Marshall, *English People in the Eighteenth Century* (London: Longmans, 1956), pp. 121–130.

24. A Lady of Rank, introduction.

25. Ibid., ch. 2.

26. Ibid., ch. 12.

27. Joan Wildblood and Peter Brenson, *The Polite World* (London: Oxford University Press, 1965), p. 243.

28. A Lady of Rank, ch. 1.

29. Marshall, p. 131.

5. THE GENTLEMAN OF RELIGION

1. Quoted by Arthur Ponsonby, *The Decline of the Aristocracy* (London: F. Fisher Unwin, 1912), p. 48.

2. Cf. Burke: "It is gone, that sensibility of principle, that chastity of honour, which felt a stain like a wound, which inspired courage while it mitigated

ferocity, which ennobled whatever it touched, and under which vice itself lost half its evil, by losing all its grossness." See Sir Philip Magnus, *Edmund Burke: A Life* (New York: Russell and Russell, 1973), p. 198.

3. Alvin Johnson, ed., "Gentleman," *The Encyclopedia of the Social Sciences,* volume 6.

4. Élie Halévy, *England in 1815* (London: Benn, 1949), Part 3.

5. Ibid.

6. Ibid.

7. Laslett, p. 52.

8. Halévy, Part 3.

9. Ibid., p. 450.

10. Ibid., p. 440.

11. Vicesimus Knox, *Essays Moral and Literary* (London: Charles Dilly, 1782), p. 160.

12. Ibid., vol. 2, p. 58.

13. See below on Dickens's gentlemen.

14. Francis Lieber, *The Character of a Gentleman* (Cincinnati: J. A. James, 1846), p. 6.

15. Ibid.

16. Ibid.

17. Ibid., p. 28.

18. Quoted by Smythe-Palmer, p. 337.

6. THE GENTLEMAN OF EDUCATION

1. Raymond Williams, *The Long Revolution* (New York: Columbia University Press, 1969), p. 128.

2. J. H. Hexter, *Reappraisals in History* (New York: Harper Torchbooks, 1961), p. 129.

3. Ibid.

4. Ibid., p. 54.

5. Williams, p. 127.

6. Hexter, p. 50.

7. Ibid., p. 53.

8. See H. C. Maxwell Lyte, cited below, for these distinctions.

9. Williams, p. 142.

10. Henry Peacham, *The Complete Gentleman,* ed. by Vergil Heltzel (Ithaca: Cornell University Press, 1962).

11. Hexter, p. 68.

12. Quoted by George C. Brauer, *The Education of a Gentleman* (New York: Bootman Associates, 1959), p. 227.

13. John Chandos, *Boys Together: English Public Schools 1800–1864* (New Haven and London: Yale University Press, 1984).

14. Daniel Defoe, *The Compleat English Gentleman,* intro. L. D. Bulbring (London, 1890).

15. Bernard Darwin, *The English Public Schools* (London: Longmans, Green, 1929), pp. 7–8.

16. H. C. Maxwell Lyte, *A History of Eton College 1440–1875* (London: Macmillan, 1875), p. 333.

17. Ibid.

18. Ibid., p. 370.

19. Chandos, p. 246.

20. Quoted by Arthur Ponsonby, p. 40.

21. See Darwin, p. 102.

22. Ibid.

23. *Edinburgh Review,* 1809, vol. 16, p. 50.

24. Ibid., p. 46.

25. Darwin, p. 116.

26. Lyte, p. 322.

27. Ibid., p. 351.

28. Wingfield-Stratford, *The Squire and His Relations,* p. 242.

29. Burn, p. 22.

30. Arthur Stanley, *The Life and Correspondence of Thomas Arnold, D.D.* (London: Murray, 1887), vol. 1, p. 97.

31. Ibid.

32. Thomas Hughes, *Tom Brown's School Days* (London: Macmillan, 1958).

33. See Stanley, vol. 2, p. 12.

34. Ibid.

35. Hughes, p. 282.

36. Lyte, p. 411.

37. Quoted by Ponsonby, p. 264.

38. Quoted by Ponsonby, p. 263.

7. INFLATIONS AND EVASIONS: THE IDEAL GENTLEMAN

1. Stephen, p. 341.

2. Ibid.

3. J. R. Vernon, *Contemporary Review,* 1869, vol. 2, p. 564.

4. Ibid., p. 561.

5. Ibid., p. 567.

6. Cf. Culler, pp. 239–240.

7. Forrester, *The Polite Philosopher,* p. 5.

8. Ibid., p. 22.

9. *The Habits of Good Society: A Handbook for Ladies and Gentlemen,* p. 48.

10. Arthur Freeling, *The Gentleman's Pocket Book of Etiquette* (Liverpool: Henry Lacey, 1838), p. 93.

11. Ibid., introduction.

12. Ibid., p. 93.

PART TWO

8. THE INFINITE NATURE OF DUTY

1. P. H. Ditchfield, *The Old English Country Squire* (London: Methuen, 1912), pp. 2–3.

2. Quoted by Thompson, p. 4.

3. Ibid.

4. Wallace Notestein, *English Folk* (Freeport, N.Y.: Books for Libraries Press, 1970), p. 51. On another model landowner in the nineteenth century see Mark Girouard, *The Victorian Country House* (New Haven: Yale University Press, 1979, pp. 2-4. Girouard discusses the "beau ideal" of the Victorian country gentleman by describing the Duke of Westminster and his devotion to his dependents.

5. Ibid., p. 68.

6. G. Kitson Clark, *The Making of Victorian England* (New York: Atheneum, 1967), p. 218.

7. Asa Briggs, *The Age of Improvement* (New York: Harper Torchbooks, 1965), p. 58.

8. Christie, p. 19.

9. Chester Kirby, *The English Country Gentleman* (London: J. Clarke, 1937), see chapter 4.

10. Ibid., p. 136.

11. Ibid.

12. Steven Marcus, *Engels, Manchester, and the Working Class* (New York: Random House, 1974), p. 169 ff.

13. For further discussion of Thackeray see Robin Gilmour, *The Idea of the Gentleman in the Victorian Novel* (London: Allen and Unwin, 1981), chapter 2.

14. In this regard, we need only recall Mr. Brooke in *Middlemarch*—the archetype of the irresponsible landholder. See also Perkin, *The Origin of Modern England 1780–1880* (London: Routledge, 1969), p. 103. *Blackwood's* expressed the following sentiments in 1820: "Everywhere, in every walk of life, it is too evident that the upper orders of Society have been tending, more and more, to a separation of themselves from those whom nature, providence, and law have placed beneath them. . . . The rich and the high have been indolently and slothfully allowing the barriers that separate them from their inferiors to increase and accumulate. . . . Men have come to deride and despise a thousand of those means of communication that in former days knit all orders of people together."

15. Bulwer-Lytton, *England and the English*, p. 31.

16. See Thompson, p. 291. See also Girouard, *The Victorian Country House*, pp. 5–6. He argues that mid-century squires were more conscientious and just than their forebears.

17. See Wingfield-Stratford, *The Squire and His Relations*, pp. 245–251.

18. Thomas MacLean, *The Old English Squire* (London: Methuen, 1904), p. 23.

19. Ibid., p. 124.

20. "The Fine Old English Gentleman" quoted by Ditchfield, p. 268.

21. Wingfield-Stratford, *The Making of a Gentleman*, ch. 10, "Civilization and the Beefs."

22. Ibid.

23. Indeed, Chaplin went broke while being the old English squire: nevertheless, he was a great deal more than a spendthrift; he was "the farmer's friend," and his reputation for generosity and goodwill was considerable. See the Marchioness of Londonderry, *Henry Chaplin* (London: Macmillan, 1926), p. 229. Lord Willoughby's remarks are not at all ambiguous: he celebrates the "squire" and his reputation.

24. See Wingfield-Stratford, *The Squire and His Relations*, pp. 349–350 for Chaplin's financial troubles.

25. Kirby, p. 146.

26. Ibid.

27. See Thompson, sect. 4, "The Life of the Landed Aristocracy."

28. Julius Gould and William Kolb, *Dictionary of Social Science* (New York: Free Press, 1964), pp. 312–313.

29. Kirby, p. 241.

30. E. W. Bovill, *The England of Nimrod and Surtees 1815–1854* (London: Oxford University Press, 1959), p. 8.

31. Ibid.

32. Bovill, ch. 14.

33. Ibid.

34. Ibid.

35. For a discussion of the negative aspects of the squire see Ditchfield, pp. 268–271. In this matter of negative criticism we should note that Dickens himself composed a squib called "The Fine Old English Gentleman" (1841): the first stanza shows that Dickens—the portrait of Wardle notwithstanding—was critical of the landed interest.

> I'll sing you a new ballad, and I'll warrant it
> first-rate,
> Of the days of the old gentleman who had that
> old estate;
> When they spent the public money at a bountiful
> old rate
> On ev'ry mistress, pimp, and scamp, at ev'ry
> noble gate
> In the fine old English Tory times;
> Soon may they come again!

Forster, *The Life of Charles Dickens* (London: Dent, 1927), vol. 1, pp. 164-165.

36. Carlyle's indictment should be compared to a jocular approach. See "A Gentleman Quite," *Bentley's Magazine,* May 1837, p. 36. This short piece of humorous verse is narrated by a "gentleman quite" who is "of no use at all." The speaker cannot—we are told—do anything but protect his quality: to sit in St. Stephen's would be "vulgar." The ending of the poem—if one can refer to such versification with the term—is rather interesting: it contains the notion that death is the most gentlemanly state—in the grave one finally discovers "graceful repose" with "No labor or toil." Thus it seems that the idea of gentility as related to death—an idea that Dickens considered in *Little Dorrit*—had, if only in humorous terms, a currency early in the nineteenth century.

9. DANDIACAL BODIES

1. Veblen, p. 11.

2. Ibid., p. 119.

3. Ibid.

4. Ibid.

5. Ellen Moers, *The Dandy* (New York: The Viking Press, 1960), pp. 32–33.

6. Dorothy George, p. 61.

7. Captain Jesse, *The Life of George Brummell, Esq.* (London: Grolier Society, n.d.), vol. 2, ch. 24.

8. Ibid., pp. 316–317.

9. Ibid., vol. 2.

10. Ibid., vol. 2, ch. 6 and vol. 1, ch. 5.

11. Elizabeth Burton, *The Pageant of Georgian England* (New York: Scribner's, 1967), ch. 8 "Of Paint, Powder, and Allied Artifices."

12. Richard Sennett, *The Fall of Public Man: On the Social Psychology of Capitalism* (New York: Vintage Books, 1978), pp. 165–166.

13. On Brummell's contempt for "business" see Jesse, vol. 1, p. 230. Brummell came into thirty thousand pounds at his majority. While he died in debt, he was never—according to Jesse—a parasite when he was in a position of favor with people of rank. This is hard to believe when we consider that he took money and goods from people in exchange for entrees into society. One man gave him five thousand pounds for such an entree: Brummell said he gave payment when he greeted the man at White's.

14. Jesse, vol. 1, p. 331.

15. Ibid., vol. 1, p. 58.

16. Ibid.

17. On Brummell's impudence see Willard Connely, *The Reign of Beau Brummell* (New York: Greystone Press, 1940), pp. 55–56.

18. Jesse, vol. 2, p. 73.

19. Quoted by Connely, p. 45.

20. Jesse, vol. 1, p. 96.

21. Connely, pp. 59–60.

22. Jesse, vol. 2, pp. 287–288.

23. The life of the snob—a life given over to calculating one's position in society and setting one's sights on a better one—is not unlike what a contemporary social scientist, W. G. Runciman, has called the "revolution of rising expectations"; according to Runciman, people see goals—rewards, status, luxury—and become discontented with their position in society because they are aware of something better, higher, more prestigious. As expectations rise, so do discontents. This social situation is clearly related to that of the snob society—a society where men and women are literally made miserable by their awareness of higher social aspirations. See Runciman, *Relative Deprivation and Social Justice* (Berkeley: University of California Press, 1966), p. 7.

24. Veblen, p. 64.

25. Phillipa Pullar, *Consuming Passions* (Boston: Little, Brown, 1970).

26. J. B. Priestley, *The Prince of Pleasure* (New York: Harper & Row, 1969), p. 186.

27. Veblen, p. 45.

28. Ditchfield, p. 193.

29. Ralph Nevill, *The Man of Pleasure* (London: Chatto and Windus, 1912), p. 28.

30. Ibid., p. 29.

31. See also J. B. Priestley, p. 46. He points out that gambling was so prevalent among the gentry and nobility in the late eighteenth century that men would "bet on anything anywhere." He quotes the betting book at Brooks's: "January 11th, 1811—Lord Alvanley bets Sir Joseph Copley twenty guineas that a certain person outlives another certain person."

32. E. Beresford Chancellor, *Memorials of St. James's Street* (London: G. Richards, 1922), pp. 122–137.

33. Ibid., p. 134.

34. For a discussion of the relationship of "deep play" to social status see Clifford Geertz, "Deep Play: Notes on the Balinese Cockfight," *Daedalus,* 1970, p. 16. Geertz brilliantly explains that what is at stake in such "playing" is "esteem, honor, dignity, respect." This is "status gambling."

35. Quoted by Chancellor, p. 209.

36. Quoted by Priestley, p. 45.

37. Mrs. Marianne (Spencer) Stanhope Hudson, *Almack's: A Novel* (London: Saunders and Otley, 1827). This work—sometimes ascribed to Charles White—takes as its major project the exposure of "the vices of the fashionable world"—among which are pride of place, contempt for "low" people, and exclusivism. A not very intelligent novel, it explores the dichotomy between honest country gentle people and London fashionables; the opening—a series of scenes in the country—contrasts solid, straightforward Mr. Mildmay ("a complete country gentleman of the old school, whose manners were polished, yet without fashion") with nouveau riche, titled people of *ton.* Shades of *Mansfield Park,* yet how different in the quality of response to the problem of integrity vs. fashion. *Almack's* trudges along in this manner for three volumes, telling us about the venality and absurdity of fashionables.

38. Ibid.

39. In the matter of sexuality and the whole underbelly of gentlemanly pleasure, see Professor Marcus's *The Other Victorians.*

40. *Real Life in London* (London: Methuen, 1905), vol. 1, p. 175.

41. Ibid.

42. Ibid., vol. 2, p. 337.

43. Ibid., vol. 2, p. 343.

44. Ibid., vol. 2, p. 147.

45. Albert Smith, *The Natural History of the Gent* (London: Kent and Co., 1847), section 3, "Chief Outward Characteristics."

46. Ibid., vol. 1.

47. Moers, p. 215.

48. Smith, vol. 6.

49. Quoted by Nevill, p. 27.

CONCLUSION

1. Lionel Trilling, *E. M. Forster* (New York: New Directions, 1943), p. 115.

2. See Richard Gill, *Happy Rural Seat: The English Country House and the Literary Imagination* (New Haven: Yale University Press, 1970), p. 153.

3. See chapter 3, endnotes 24 and 25, for references to Trilling and Annan; E. M. Forster's memoir *Marianne Thornton* is discussed in Trilling's essay. Trilling gives a concise picture of the Clapham sect and their values. On Keynes, see Paul Levy, *Moore: G. E. Moore and the Cambridge Apostles* (New York: Holt, Rinehart and Winston, 1980).

4. Levy, p. 26.

5. Ibid., pp. 1–9.

6. Ibid., pp. 241–242.

7. See Paul Johnson, *Modern Times: The World From the Twenties to the Eighties* (New York: Harper & Row, Publishers, 1983), p. 172.

8. For a consideration of the opposite point of view, which holds that the Communist is the man of duty, see Michael Straight's treatment of the poet John Cornford in *After Long Silence* (New York: W. W. Norton, 1983), p. 73. "John inherited a keen sense of personal honor from his father, a Classical scholar. He believed in the Communist party as a contemporary expression of that sense of honor and obligation. He saw it as a cleansing force in his own time as well as in some future era. He treasures it as a human experience, not the instrument of some vast historic trend."

9. Raven continues in the tradition of writers who explore the public school as character factory and key determinant in the formation of gentlemanly values. Charterhouse formed the gentleman; Kings, Cambridge the intellectual.

10. Philip Mason, *The English Gentleman: The Rise and Fall of an Ideal* (New York: William Morrow and Company, 1982), p. 227.

11. Gill, especially the introduction, "The Quest for Community," pp. 1–19.

12. Shirley Letwin, *The Gentleman in Trollope: Individuality and Moral Conduct* (Cambridge: Harvard University Press, 1982), ch. 1.

13. Mark Girouard, *Life in the English Country House: A Social and Architectural History* (New Haven: Yale University Press, 1978), p. 318.

14. Ibid.

15. Ibid.

SELECTED SOURCES

Addison, Joseph. *The Sir Roger de Coverley Papers.* New York: American Book Company, 1904.

Annan, Noel. "The Intellectual Aristocracy," in *Studies in History,* ed. by J. H. Plumb. New York: Longmans, Green, 1955.

Ashton, John. *England Under the Regency.* London: Chatto and Windus, 1899.

Austen, Jane. *Persuasion.* Baltimore: Penguin Books, 1967.

———. *Pride and Prejudice.* New York: Norton, 1966.

Bagehot, Walter. *The English Constitution.* London: Oxford University Press, 1958.

Barron, Oswald. "The Gentility of Richard Barker," *The Ancestor,* vol. 2 (July 1902), 48–54.

Bluett, J. C. *Duelling and the Laws of Honour Explained.* London: Seeley and Burnside, 1835.

Bovill, E. W. *The England of Nimrod and Surtees 1815–1854.* London: Oxford University Press, 1959.

———. *English Country Life.* London: Oxford University Press, 1962.

Brauer, George C. *The Education of a Gentleman.* New York: Bookman Associates, 1959.

Briggs, Asa. *The Age of Improvement.* New York: Harper Torchbooks, 1965.

———. *Victorian People.* New York: Harper & Row, 1963.

The British Code of the Duel. London: Knight and Lacey, 1824.

Bryant, Arthur. *The Age of Elegance 1812–1822.* New York: Harper, 1950.

Bulwer-Lytton, Edward George. *England and the English,* 2 vols. London: Bentley, 1833.

———. *Pelham; or the Adventures of a Gentleman,* 2 vols. Philadelphia: Lippincott, 1886.

Burn, W. L. *The Age of Equipoise.* New York: Norton, 1965.

Burton, Elizabeth. *The Pageant of Georgian England*. New York: Scribner's, 1967.

Cady, Edwin. *The Gentleman in America*. Syracuse: Syracuse University Press, 1949.

Calvert, George H. *The Gentleman*. Boston: Ticknor and Fields, 1863.

Carlyle, Thomas. *Latter Day Pamphlets*. London: Chapman and Hall, 1885.

————. *Past and Present*. Boston: Riverside, 1965.

————. *Sartor Resartus*. London: Dent, 1959.

Castiglione, Baldassar. *The Courtier*. New York: Anchor Books, 1959.

Cecil, David. *Lord Melbourne*. New York: Grosset and Dunlap, 1954.

Chancellor, G. Beresford. *Memorials of St. James's Street*. London: G. Richards, 1922.

Chandos, John. *Boys Together: English Public Schools 1800–1864*. New Haven and London: Yale University Press, 1984.

"The Character of the English Gentleman," *The Gentleman's Magazine* 45 (1795), 309–310.

Chesterton, G. K. *The Victorian Age in Literature*. London: Oxford University Press, 1966.

Christie, O. F. *Transition from Aristocracy, 1852–1867*. London: Seeley, Service and Co., 1922.

Connely, Willard. *The Reign of Beau Brummell*. New York: Greystone Press, 1940.

Craik, Mrs. [Dinah Mullock]. *John Halifax, Gentleman*. New York: Harper Brothers, 1859.

Culler, Dwight. *The Imperial Intellect*. New Haven: Yale University Press, 1955.

Darwin, Bernard. *The English Public Schools*. London: Longmans, Green, 1929.

Defoe, Daniel. *The Complete English Gentleman*, intro. L. O. Bulbring. London, 1890.

Dickens and the Carpenter: Six Letters from Charles Dickens to John A. Owens. Philadelphia: Free Library, 1947.

Dickens, Charles. *The New Oxford Illustrated Dickens*. London: Oxford University Press, 1948–1958.

Disraeli, Benjamin. *Sybil*. London: Oxford University Press, 1964.

Ditchfield, P. H. *The Old English Country Squire*. London: Methuen, 1914.

Dupee, F. W., ed. *The Selected Letters of Charles Dickens*. New York: Farrar, Straus and Cudahy, 1960.

Edinburgh Review, 16 (1809), 45–50.

Egan, Pierce. *Real Life in London*. 2 vols. London: Methuen, 1905.

The English Gentleman: His Principles, His Feelings, His Manner, His Pursuits.
London: Bell, 1849.

Escott, T. H. S. *England: Its People, Polity and Pursuits.* London: Chapman and
Hall, 1885.

Etiquette for Gentlemen With Hints on the Art of Conversation. London: Telt
and Bogue, 1841.

Faber, Richard. *Proper Stations: Class in Victorian Fiction.* London: Faber and
Faber, Ltd., 1971.

Fielding, Henry. *Jonathan Wild.* New York: Signet Classics, 1961.

Forrester, James. *The Polite Philosopher.* London: J. Wilson, 1736.

Forster, E. M. *Howards End.* New York: Alfred Knopf, 1943.

————. *The Longest Journey.* New York: Alfred Knopf, 1922.

Forster, John. *The Life of Charles Dickens.* New York: Doubleday Doran, 1928.

Freeling, Arthur. *The Gentleman's Pocket Book of Etiquette.* Liverpool: Henry
Lacey, 1838.

Friswell, H. *The Gentle Life.* London: Simpson, Law, Son and Marston, 1868.

Geertz, Clifford. "Deep Play: Notes on the Balinese Cockfight," *Daedalus* (1970),
1–37.

The Gentleman: A Satire. London: Baldwin, Cradock and Joy, 1818.

"A Gentleman Quite," *Bentley's Magazine* (May 1937), 36.

George, Dorothy. *Hogarth to Cruikshank: Social Change in Graphic Satire.* New
York: Walker, 1967.

Gilchrist, J. *A Brief Display of the Origins and Hisotry of Ordeals.* London:
W. Bulmer and W. Nicol, 1821.

Gill, Richard. *Happy Rural Seat.* New Haven: Yale University Press, 1972.

Gilmour, Robin. *The Idea of The Gentleman in the Victorian Novel.* London:
Allen and Unwin, 1981.

Girouard, Mark. *Life in the English Country House; A Social and Architectual
History.* New Haven: Yale University Press, 1978.

————. *The Return to Camelot: Chivalry and the English Gentleman.* New Haven:
Yale University Press, 1981.

————. *The Victorian Country House.* New Haven: Yale University Press,
1979.

Gould, Julius, and William Kolb. *Dictionary of Social Science.* New York: Free
Press, 1964.

Gretton, R. H. *The English Middle Class.* London: G. Bell and Sons, 1919.

Gronow, Captain. *Reminiscences and Recollections of Captain Gronow.* London:
Nimmo, 1886.

Grossmith, George. *The Diary of a Nobody.* London: Dent, 1962.

Guttsman, W. L. *The English Ruling Class*. London: Weidenfeld and Nicholson, 1969.

The Habits of Good Society: A Handbook for Ladies and Gentlemen. London: James Hogg and Sons, 1860.

Halévy, Élie. *England in 1815*. London: Benn, 1949.

Hexter, J. H. *Reappraisals in History*. New York: Harper Torchbooks, 1961.

Hood, Paxton. *A Perfect Gentleman*. Delivered in Brighton Pavilion before the YMCA, February 21, 1872.

Houghton, Walter. *The Victorian Frame of Mind*. New Haven: Yale University Press, 1957.

House, Humphry. *The Dickens World*. London: Oxford University Press, 1965.

Hudson, Derek. *Munby: Man of Two Worlds*. Boston: Gambit, 1972.

Hudson, Marianne (Spencer) Stanhope. *Almack's: A Novel*, 3 vols. London: Saunders and Otley, 1827.

Hughes, Thomas. *Memoir of a Brother*. London: Macmillan, 1873.

————. *Tom Brown's School Days*. London: Macmillan and Co., Ltd., 1958.

Jesse, Captain William. *The Life of George Brummell, Esq.*, 2 vols. London: Groiler Society, n.d.

Johnson, Alvin, and R. A. Seligman, ed. *The Encyclopedia of the Social Sciences*. New York: Macmillan, 1930.

Johnson, Edgar. *Charles Dickens: His Tragedy and Triumph*, 2 vols. New York: Simon and Schuster, 1952.

Johnson, Paul. *Modern Times: The World from the Twenties to the Eighties*. New York: Harper & Row, 1983.

Johnson, Ben. "To Penshurst," *Seventeenth Century English Poetry*, ed. Miriam Starkman. New York: Knopf, 1967, vol. 2, pp. 32–34.

Kelso, Ruth. *The Doctrine of the English Gentleman in the Sixteenth Century*. Urbana: University of Illinois Press, 1929.

Kingsley, Henry. *Ravenshoe*, ed. with intro. by William Scheurle. Lincoln: University of Nebraska Press, 1967.

Kirby, Chester. *The English Country Gentleman*. London: J. Clarke, 1937.

Kitson-Clark, G. *The Making of Victorian England*. New York: Atheneum, 1967.

Knox, Vicesimus. *Essays Moral and Literary*. London: Charles Dilly, 1782.

A Lady of Rank (C. W. Day). *Hints on Etiquette*. London: Longmans, 1861.

Larkin, Philip. *Jill*. Woodstock, N.Y.: The Overlook Press, 1984.

Lascelles, Edward C. *Life of Charles James Fox*. Rpt. New York: Octagon Books, 1970.

Laski, Harold. *The Danger of Being a Gentleman*. New York: Viking, 1940.

Laslett, Peter. *The World We Have Lost.* New York: Scribner's, 1965.

Lawrence, D. H. *Lady Chatterley's Lover,* with an afterword by Harry T. Moore. New York: New American Library, 1962.

Lawrence, Sir James. *On the Nobility of the British Gentry.* Paris: A. W. Galignani, 1828.

Lee, Patricia Ann. "The Ideal of the English Gentleman in the 17th Century." Dissertation, Columbia University, 1966.

Letwin, Shirley. *The Gentleman in Trollope: Individuality and Moral Conduct.* Cambridge, Mass.: Harvard University Press, 1982.

Lewis, Roy, and Angus Maude. *The English Middle Classes.* London: Phoenix House, 1949.

Lieber, Francis. *The Character of a Gentleman.* Cincinnati: J. A. James, 1846.

Londonderry, Edith Helen (Chaplin). *Henry Chaplin.* London: Macmillan, 1926.

Lyte, H. C. Maxwell. *A History of Eton College 1440–1875.* London: Macmillan, 1875.

Macaulay, Thomas Babington. *The History of England,* ed. by Hugh Trevor-Roper. New York: Washington Square Press, 1968.

Mack, Edward. *Public Schools and British Opinion 1780–1860.* London: Methuen, 1938.

MacLean, Thomas. *The Old English Squire.* London: Methuen, 1905.

Magnus, Sir Philip. *Edmund Burke: A Life.* New York: Russell and Russell, 1973.

"Manners and Customs of Ye English," *Punch,* 1849.

Marcus, Steven. *Dickens From Pickwick to Dombey.* New York: Simon and Schuster, 1968.

————. *Engels, Manchester, and The Working Class.* New York: Random House, 1974.

————. *The Other Victorians.* New York: Basic Books, 1965.

Margetson, Stella. *Leisure and Pleasure in the Nineteenth Century.* New York: Coward, McCann, 1969.

Markham, Felix. *Oxford.* London: Weidenfeld and Nicholson, 1967.

Marshall, Dorothy. *English People in the Eighteenth Century.* London: Longmans, 1956.

Marx, Karl. *The Basic Writings on Politics and Philosophy,* ed. by Lewis Feuer. New York: Anchor, 1969.

————. *Economic and Philosophic Manuscripts.* New York: International Publishers, 1973.

Mason, J. E. *Gentlefolk in the Making: Studies in the History of English Courtesy Literature and Related Topics from 1531–1774.* Philadelphia: University of Pennsylvania Press, 1935.

Mason, Philip. *The English Gentleman: The Rise and Fall of an Ideal.* New York: William Morrow and Lamparey, 1982.

McMaster, R. D. "The Dandy and the Savage," *Studies in the Novel,* vol. 1 (1969), no. 2, 133–145.

————. "Society (Whatever That Was): Dickens and Society as an Abstraction," *Etudes Anglaises,* 23 (1970), 125–135.

Mill, J. S. *Essays on Politics and Culture,* ed. by Gertrude Himmelfarb. New York: Anchor, 1963.

Millingen, J. G. *The History of Duelling.* London: Bentley, 1841.

Mingay, G. *English Landed Society in the Eighteenth Century.* London: Routledge and Kegan Paul, 1963.

Moers, Ellen. *The Dandy.* New York: The Viking Press, 1960.

Moore, G. E. *Principia Ethica.* Cambridge: Cambridge University Press, 1959.

Namier, Sir Lewis. *England in the Age of the American Revolution.* New York: St. Martin's Press, 1961.

Nevill, Ralph. *The Man of Pleasure.* London: Chatto and Windus, 1912.

Newman, J. H. *The Idea of University.* New York: Image Books, 1959.

Newsome, David. *Godliness and Good Learning: Four Studies on a Victorian Ideal.* London: Murray, 1961.

Nicholson, Harold. *Good Behaviour: Being a Study of Certain Types of Civility.* Boston: Beacon Press, 1960.

Nimrod (C. J. Apperley). *Memoirs of the Life of John Mytton, Esq.* London: Kegan Paul, Trench and Trubner, 1834.

Notestein, Wallace. *English Folk.* Freeport, N.Y.: Books for Libraries Press, 1970.

Orwell, George. "Charles Dickens," *A Collection of Essays.* New York: Anchor, 1954, pp. 55–111.

Peachum, Henry. *The Complete Gentleman,* ed. by Vergil Heltzel. Ithaca: Cornell University Press, 1962.

Pearsall, Ronald. *The Worm in the Bud.* Toronto: Macmillan, 1969.

Perkin, Harold. *The Origin of Modern England 1780–1880.* London: Routledge, 1969.

Polanyi, Karl. *The Great Transformation.* Boston: Beacon Press, 1957.

Ponsonby, Arthur. *The Decline of the Aristocracy*. London: F. Fisher Unwin, 1912.

Priestley, J. B. *The Prince of Pleasure*. New York: Harper & Row, 1969.

Pullar, Phillipa. *Consuming Passions*. Boston: Little, Brown, 1970.

Quinlan, Maurice. *The Victorian Prelude*. New York: Columbia University, 1941.

Raven, Simon. *The English Gentleman*. London: Anthony Blond, 1961.

Reader, W. J. *Professional Men: The Rise of the Professional Classes in the Nineteenth Century*. London: Weidenfeld and Nicholson, 1966.

Reed, John. *Old School Ties: The Public School in British Literature*. Syracuse: Syracuse University Press, 1964.

Richardson, Samuel. *Sir Charles Grandison*. Philadelphia: J. B. Lippincott, 1902.

Rosa, Matthew. *The Silver Fork Novels*. New York: Columbia University Press, 1936.

Round, J. Horace. *Peerage and Pedigree*. London: Nisbet and Co., 1910.

Routh, H. V. *England Under Victoria*. New York: Harcourt, Brace, 1931.

—————. *Money, Morals, and Manners as Revealed in Modern Literature*. London: Nicholson and Watson, 1935.

Routledge's Etiquette for Gentlemen. London: Routledge, 1965.

Runciman, W. G. *Relative Deprivation and Social Justice*. Berkeley: University of California Press, 1966.

Ruskin, John. *The Genius of John Ruskin,* ed. John D. Rosenberg. Boston: Riverside, 1963.

Sackville-West, Vita. *The Edwardians*. New York: Doubleday, 1930.

Samuel, Maurice. *The Gentleman and the Jew*. New York: Knopf, 1952.

Scott, Walter. *Rob Roy*. Philadelphia: Lippincott, 1879.

Sedgewick, Henry Dwight. *In Praise of Gentlemen*. Boston: Little, Brown, and Company, 1935.

Sells, David, ed. *The International Encyclopedia of the Social Sciences*. New York: Macmillan and the Free Press, 1968.

Sennett, Richard. *The Fall of Public Man: On the Social Psychology of Capitalism*. New York: Vintage Books, 1978.

Simpson, Alfred. *The Book of Etiquette or the Whole Art of Politeness*. Manchester: Heywood, 1841.

Sitwell, Sir George. *The Ancestor,* 1902, pp. 69–70.

Smiles, Samuel. *Self-Help, With Illustrations of Conduct and Character*. New York: John Ballin, 1887.

Smith, Albert. *The Natural History of the Gent.* London: Kent and Co., 1847.

Smollett, Tobias. *Humphry Clinker.* Baltimore: Penguin, 1967.

Smythe-Palmer, A. *The Ideal of a Gentleman.* London: Routledge, 1908.

Stanley, Arthur. *The Life and Correspondence of Thomas Arnold, D.D.,* 2 vols. London: Murray, 1887.

Stephen, Fitzjames. *Cornhill Magazine,* 5 (1862), 327–343.

Stephen, Leslie, and Sidney Lee. *The Dictionary of National Biography.* London: Oxford University Press, 1921.

Stone, Lawrence. *The Crisis of the Aristocracy.* London: Oxford University Press, 1967.

Straight, Michael. *After Long Silence.* New York: W. W. Norton & Co., 1983.

Sykes, Christopher. *Four Studies in Loyalty.* New York: Sloane Associates, 1946.

Talbot, Laura. *The Gentlewomen.* New York: Penguin Books, 1985.

Tennyson, Alfred Lord. "The Princess," *The Poems and Plays of Alfred Lord Tennyson.* New York: Modern Library, 1938, 221–222.

Thackeray, William Makepeace. *Barry Lyndon.* Lincoln: University of Nebraska, 1962.

————. *The Book of Snobs.* London: Smith, Elder and Co., 1872.

————. *The Four Georges.* New York: Dolphin Books, n.d.

————. *Mr. Brown's Letters to a Young Man About Town.* New York: D. Appleton and Co., 1853.

————. *Pendennis.* London: Dent, 1959.

————. *A Shabby Genteel Story and Other Tales.* New York: Appleton and Co., 1852.

————. *Vanity Fair.* Baltimore: Penguin, 1972.

————. *The Yellowplush Papers.* New York: D. Appleton and Co., 1864.

Thompson, F. M. L. *English Landed Society in the Nineteenth Century.* London: Routledge and Kegan Paul, 1963.

Thrupp, Sylvia. *The Merchant Class of Medieval London.* Ann Arbor: University of Michigan Press, 1961.

Tocqueville, Alexis de. *Democracy in America,* ed. by Richard Heffner. New York: New American Library, 1956.

————. *Journey to England and Ireland,* trans. by George Lawrence and K. P. Mayers. New Haven: Yale University Press, 1958.

Trevelyan, G. O. *The Early Life of Charles James Fox.* New York: Harper and Brothers, 1901.

Trilling, Lionel. *A Gathering of Fugitives.* Boston: Beacon Press, 1956.

————. *E. M. Forster.* New York: New Directions, 1943.

———. *The Liberal Imagination.* New York: Doubleday, 1950.

———. *The Opposing Self.* New York: Viking, 1959.

———. *Sincerity and Authenticity.* Cambridge, Mass.: Harvard University Press, 1972.

True Politeness or Etiquette for Everyone. London: Orr, 1840.

The True Science of Etiquette or, An Exposition of the Principles of Real Etiquette. Glasgow: Robert Stuart, 1836.

Van Doren, Carl. *The Oxford Dictionary of Quotations.* London: Oxford University Press, 1941.

Veblen, Thorsten. *The Theory of the Leisure Class.* New York: 1953.

Vernon, J. R. *Contemporary Review,* 2 (1869), 561–580.

Wagner, Sir Anthony. *Heralds and Heraldry in the Middle Ages.* London: Oxford University Press, 1939.

Weber, Max. *Basic Concepts in Sociology.* New York: Citadel, 1969.

———. *Essays in Sociology,* ed. and trans. by H. H. Gerth and C. Wright Mills. New York: Oxford University Press, 1946.

Wildblood, Joan, and Peter Brenson. *The Polite World.* London: Oxford University Press, 1965.

Wilkinson, Rupert. *Gentlemanly Power: British Leadership and the Public School Tradition.* London: Oxford University Press, 1973.

Williams, Raymond. *The Long Revolution.* New York: Columbia University Press, 1961.

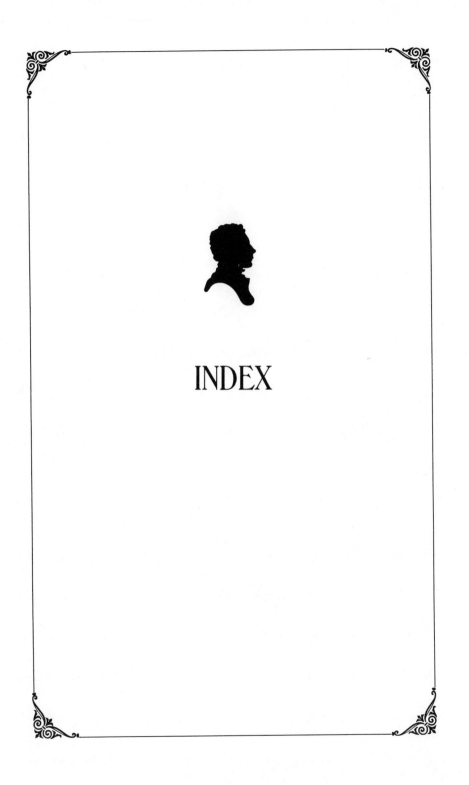

INDEX

INDEX

and Smollett, 42–44
and social harmony, 40

Wealth
 and ancestry, 15
 and aristocracy, 16
 and Austen, 87–88
 and conduct, patterns of, 19
 and democracy, 16–17
 importance of, 16
 and number of gentleman, 19
 processes of, to becoming gentleman, 14–16
 and social mobility, 14
Weber, Max, 11
Westminister (school), 111

Wilcox, Charles (fictional), 120–21
Wild, Jonathan, 20, 25
William of Wykeham, 36, 53
Williams, Raymond, 53
Will Wimble, 82
Wilson, A. N., 132
Wimble, Will, 82
Winchester (school), 53
Wingfield-Stratford, Esme
 and breeding, 31, 33
 and duty of gentleman, 84, 86
Winter, Sir Leslie (fictional), 122–23
Wrayburn, Eugene, 51
Wykeham, William of, 36, 53

Yellowplush Papers (Thackeray), 104–
 5, 109